THE
CHICANO
HERITAGE

THE AMERICAN OCCUPATION
OF NEW MEXICO
1821-1852

SISTER MARY LOYOLA

ARNO PRESS

A New York Times Company

New York — 1976

Editorial Supervision: LESLIE PARR

---◆---

Reprint Edition 1976 by Arno Press Inc.

Copyright © 1939 by the
  Historical Society of New Mexico

Reprinted by permission of the
  New Mexico Historical Review
  and Sister Mary Loyola

Reprinted from a copy in the State
  Historical Society of Wisconsin Library

THE CHICANO HERITAGE
ISBN for complete set: 0-405-09480-9
See last pages of this volume for titles.

Manufactured in the United States of America

---◆---

Library of Congress Cataloging in Publication Data

Mary Loyola, Sister, 1889-
    The American occupation of New Mexico, 1821-1852.

    (The Chicano heritage)
    Reprint of the ed. published by the University of
New Mexico Press, Albuquerque, which was issued as
v. 8 of Publications in history of the Historical
Society of New Mexico.
    Bibliography: p.
    1. New Mexico--History. I. Title. II. Series.
III. Series: New Mexico. Historical Society.
Publications in history ; v. 8.
F800.M37 1976   978.9'03   76-1281
ISBN 0-405-09512-0

HISTORICAL SOCIETY OF NEW MEXICO

PUBLICATIONS IN HISTORY

VOL. VIII   SEPTEMBER, 1939

THE AMERICAN OCCUPATION OF NEW MEXICO 1821-1852

SISTER MARY LOYOLA, S.H.N., PH.D.
College of the Holy Names
Oakland, California

THE UNIVERSITY OF NEW MEXICO PRESS

ALBUQUERQUE

CONTENTS

TO
C. S. H. N.

PREFACE

During more than a quarter of a century prior to the Treaty of Guadalupe-Hidalgo, 1848, by which New Mexico became a part of the United States, American interest in this section of the Mexican dominions had been steadily increasing. At the outbreak of the Mexican War, the conquest of this coveted region formed an integral part of the policy of the United States.

This monograph attempts to indicate the place of New Mexico in the westward movement; to show why it was considered of such vital significance to the United States; and to manifest the important role that it played in national politics during and immediately after the war. A brief discussion of internal affairs and their national consequences immediately after the conquest is also included.

The source materials used for this work were made accessible to me through the generosity of several owners of collections of manuscripts, and of librarians in various places. The United States Government Documents and the official correspondence of Indian Agents connected with New Mexico form part of the Bancroft Library of the University of California; Dr. H. E. Bolton supplied invaluable material from his personal collection of transcripts from the principal Archives of Mexico; the late Mr. Benjamin M. Read of Santa Fe allowed me to use freely his private collection of manuscripts and documents; Mr. Lansing Bloom and his able assistants opened to me the State Archives of New Mexico at Santa Fe as well as the collections of the Historical Society of New Mexico; Mr. F. T. Cheetham of Taos, N. M., gave me valued suggestions regarding local traditions; and Capt. R. B. Haselden, Curator of Manuscripts, Huntington Library, San Marino, California, directed my attention to the Ritch Collection which had been recently acquired by the Library from the Catron Estate of Santa Fe. The helpful courtesy of the members of the Historical

Society of New Mexico, especially of Mr. Paul A. F. Walter, President, and of Mr. Lansing Bloom, Secretary, was unfailing.

It is a pleasure to have this opportunity to express my sincere appreciation of the assistance given by these and others who have helped to make this work possible. Foremost among these is Dr. H. E. Bolton whose deep erudition, unfailing enthusiasm, and kindly interest, have been a continued source of inspiration and encouragement. Sincere thanks are due to Dr. H. I. Priestley whose scholarly direction in earlier graduate study was of inestimable value. My indebtedness is great for the generous encouragement of my associates, the members of the Congregation of the Sisters of the Holy Names of Jesus and Mary.

THE AMERICAN OCCUPATION OF NEW MEXICO
1821-1852

By Sister Mary Loyola, S.H.N., Ph.D.

Chapter I

The Anglo-American Pioneer Movement

NEW MEXICO, which perpetuates in its name the hope of the early Spanish explorers to find in this northern region a civilization rivaling in splendor that of the Aztecs of the south, seems always to have had some inherent charm which piqued the curiosity and excited the interest of the foreigner. Shortly after Spain had taken possession of the territory, efforts were made by French adventurers to gain access to this land of reputed wealth in gold and silver and opportunities for trade. As early as 1703 a band of twenty Canadians went from the Illinois country for the purpose of trading and learning about the mines.[1]

Spain, doubtless, had a foreboding that through just such means as this her colonial empire would be wrested from her or her heirs. Therefore in 1723, royal orders in consonance with the general colonial policy prohibited the trade which the Spaniards were carrying on with the French in Louisiana.[2] Sometimes enforced, sometimes neglected, such mandates did not prevent continued attempts to develop intercourse during the French occupation of Louisiana.[3]

Posts were erected in the intervening territory; repeated efforts were made to establish peace between the various Indian tribes whose internecine strife rendered French ingress difficult or impossible. Between 1718 and 1739 trappers and adventurers vied with one another in at-

---

1. Bolton and Marshall, *The Colonization of North America*, 282-5.
2. Bancroft, H. H., *Arizona and New Mexico*, 238.
3. Bolton, H. E., *Athanase de Mézières and the Louisiana-Texas Frontier*, I, 49 *et seq.*

tempts to push up the Missouri and thence to New Mexico. At the latter date, the Mallet party succeeded not only in reaching the ambitioned destination, but also in returning alive. They reported good prospects for trade.

In 1741 a futile attempt to reach the Mexican outposts was initiated by Governor Bienville of Louisiana. In 1746 or 1747 a treaty between the Comanche and the Jumano Indians made the Arkansas route safe. The immediate consequence was the entrance into Spanish territory of Frenchmen who, as early as 1748, went, thirty-one strong, to trade muskets for mules with the Comanches. The members of this party did not enter Santa Fé; but in the ensuing years, one group after another went or was taken to the capital of New Mexico. Governor Velez finally advised the Viceroy to forbid those who thus came to return to the French settlements. Thus, he thought, further information about New Mexico which would encourage others to try their fortune in the foreign land would not be disseminated. Moreover their knowledge of various crafts would be an asset to a place which evidently suffered much from lack of skilled workmen.

However, repeated intrusions were being effected at times with the approval or connivance of French officials. An almost identical situation was also developing on the Texas-Louisiana frontier. Reports from both areas resulted in a royal decree of June 1751 whereby it was ordered "that French intruders in the Spanish dominions be prevented from returning to their country under any pretext whatsoever." The Viceroy was ordered to keep vigilant watch of the operations of the French nation.[4]

With the definite cession of Louisiana to Spain (1762) fear of foreign intrusion into New Mexico was practically removed. By order of the Viceroy of New Spain the path between Santa Fé and St. Louis was now officially explored by the Frenchman, Vial, in 1792-1793.[5] While extensive

4. Bolton, H. E., "French Intrusions into New Mexico" in *The Pacific Ocean History*, 389-407. Dr. Bolton used as his source two *expedientes* which he discovered in the archives of Mexico.

5. Bolton, H. E., *Texas in the Middle Eighteenth Century*, 132; Houck, L., *The Spanish Regime in Missouri*, I, 350.

trade was not, perhaps, carried on between the two places, it would seem strange if it had completely ceased. The casual observations of Lewis and Clark in regard to such intercourse lead one to infer that such trading was not unknown.[6]
Preliminary Steps in Gaining Access to New Mexico.
Almost half a century before any official attempt was made by the United States to take forcible possession of New Mexico, beginnings of the extension of American influence into the region were made by means of commerce. Scarcely had the Louisiana territory been acquired when attempts were made to break through the barriers set up by Spanish law to the entrance of foreigners into the Internal Provinces of which New Mexico formed a part. This was but one phase of the widespread movement of the sturdy frontiersmen and adventurous trappers to explore the new land west of the Mississippi and force it to yield up its riches to their determined efforts.[7]

Baptiste La Lande, a French creole, has acquired a scarcely deserved fame because of the fact that he made the first recorded expedition from American soil to Santa Fé. He was sent out in 1804 by Wm. Morrison of Kaskaskia to trade with the Pawnees, and, if possible, to make his way to Santa Fé to observe the prospects of opening up trade.[8] La Lande sent some Indians ahead to determine what sort of welcome would await him. As a result, the Spaniards came out to where he was stationed and accompanied him into the province. "Finding that the goods sold high, that lands were offered him and that the women were kind, he concluded to expatriate himself and convert the property of Morrison to his own benefit."[9]

---

6. Chittenden, H. M., *The History of the American Fur Trade of the Far West,* II, 490.
7. See Chittenden, *op. cit., passim.*
8. Pike, Z. M., *Exploratory Travels* (Rees ed.), 263.
9. *Ibid.,* 250. Chittenden says that the government lent its assistance to keep La Lande by offering him land "doubtless preferring that he should stay, rather than return with reports which would inevitably lead to a renewal of the enterprise." (Chittenden, *op. cit.,* II, 390.)

Morrison took advantage of Pike's official expedition to the Red River to attempt to recover his goods. The endeavor to obtain satisfaction was unsuccessful, and La Lande remained in Santa Fé "not only unmolested but honored and esteemed till his death, which occurred some fifteen or twenty years afterward—leaving a large family and sufficient property to entitle him to the fame of 'rico' among his neighbors."[10]

The next enterprise of similar nature under American auspices, of which we have any information, was that undertaken by James Purcell, a native of Baird's Town, Kentucky. Then, as later, American energy would not be daunted by the dangers to be incurred because of the savage tribes which surrounded the regions through which the path to New Mexico lay, or the physical hardships that must necessarily be endured, or the laws of Spain which forbade foreign trade.[11] Before La Lande's adventure, Purcell, in 1802, with two companions left St. Louis for the West where they hunted and trapped. While they were preparing to descend the Arkansas to New Orleans, their horses were stolen by the hostile Kansas Indians. Their determined efforts to recover the animals so astounded the Indians that they dubbed the trappers the "Mad Americans," and in admiration returned the stolen horses. Hardships continued until, finally, their whole year's labor was rendered futile by the loss of all their peltries. Purcell then joined a chance acquaintance who was going toward the Mandan villages. There he was employed with some Indian bands in a hunting and trading expedition.

The Indians desired to trade with the Spaniards, so they sent Purcell and his companions with two of their own number to Santa Fé to negotiate the matter for them. The governor, Alencaster, granted the request and the Indians returned to their bands. But Purcell took advantage of this

---

10. Gregg, J., *Commerce of the Prairies* I, 18. La Lande was buried at Rancho de Taos. (Note supplied by F. T. Cheatham of Taos).

11. See Willard, "Inland Trade with New Mexico" in *Personal Narrative of James O. Pattie*, 257.

opportunity to enjoy civilized companions once more and took up his abode in Santa Fé (1805) where he pursued his trade of carpenter with great success. He confided to Pike, who met him there, that though a passport would be given to him on demand, he was obliged to give security that he would not leave the country without permission, and that he was not allowed to write; that he had found gold at the head of the Platte river and feared his refusal to reveal the place where it was found, since he believed it to be in American territory, would be an obstacle to his return.[12] Although this enterprise had practically no effect upon commerce, it is of interest as a proof of American hardihood.[13]

The most important of the early expeditions to Santa Fé was that undertaken by Lieutenant Zebulon Montgomery Pike in 1806-7. Instructions were issued by the War Department ordering him to bring about a peace between the Kansas and Osage Indians, and to effect an interview and establish friendly relations with the Ietans and Comanches. Since this would probably lead Pike close to the Spanish settlements of New Mexico, he was cautioned to be on his guard not to cause alarm or give offense, since "the affairs of Spain and the United States appear to be on the point of amicable adjustment and, moreover, it is the desire of the President to cultivate the friendship and harmonious intercourse of all the nations of the earth, and particularly our nearest neighbors, the Spaniards." Pike was ordered to make careful scientific observations and to keep a precise record of distances traversed and of the general character of the country.[14]

Many who have studied carefully the circumstances attendant upon Pike's expedition are convinced that there was much more in his instructions than appears in the documents. Coues says:

12. Pike, Z. M., *Exploratory Travels* (Rees Ed.) 345-348. "The spelling Purcell is undoubtedly correct although Pike gives it as Pursley" (Chittenden, II, 493).

13. Pino, P. B., *Noticas Historicas y Estadisticas*, 74.

14. Wilkinson, J., *To Lieutenant Z. M. Pike, July 12, 1806. Document of War Dept.* Cited by Rees, p. XIII-XIV.

It is well understood that Pike had secret instructions from the traitor, Gen. Wilkinson, over and beyond those which were ostensible; and no doubt the main purpose of his expedition was to open the way to Santa Fé, with reference to such military operations as then seemed probable. It is certain that General Wilkinson contemplated the possibility if not probability of invading New Mexico.[15]

Gregg, on the other hand states:

Many will believe and assert to the present day, however, that this expedition had some connection with the famous project of Aaron Burr; yet the noble and patriotic character of the officer who conducted it will not permit us to countenance such an aspersion.[16]

The interesting details of Pike's trip were carefully recorded by himself, and need not be repeated here. His erection of a fort on the west side of what he thought was the Red River, but which was in reality the Rio Grande and therefore unquestionably in Spanish territory, caused the authorities of New Mexico to send a body of cavalry to conduct him, by force if necessary, to Santa Fé. If his real object was to reach this Spanish capital, it was thus accomplished in the most advantageous manner; for in his enforced stay and travels in New Spain, he had sufficient opportunity to observe conditions closely and yet he was allowed to return to the United States.

His account of the forbidden land aroused enthusiasm among his countrymen, and was doubtless the cause of the fitting up of many later trading expeditions. They ignored his reports of the difficulties to be encountered, and considered only the advantages to be gained. He states:

These vast plains of the western hemisphere may become in time equally celebrated with the

---

15.   Coues, Elliott (ed.) *The Expeditions of Zebulon Montgomery Pike*, II, 563-4.
      See also Chittenden, H. M., *The American Fur Trade of the Far West*, II, 494.
and Bancroft, H. H., *Arizona and New Mexico*, 295.
16.   Gregg, J., *Commerce of the Prairies*, I, 19.

sandy deserts of Africa, for 1 saw in my route in
various places, tracts of many leagues where the
wind had thrown up the sand, in all the fanciful
forms of the ocean's rolling waves, and on which
not a speck of vegetation existed. But from these
immense prairies may arise one great advantage;
the restriction of our population to some certain
limits, and thereby a continuation of the Union.
Our citizens being so prone to rambling and ex-
tending themselves on the frontier, will, through
necessity, be constrained to limit their extent on
the west to the borders of the Missouri and Mississippi, while they leave the prairies, incapable of
cultivation, to the wandering and uncivilized aborigines of the country.[17]

He describes Santa Fé, the population of which he
estimated at 4,500, as

. . . situated along the banks of a small creek
which comes down from the mountains and runs
west to the Rio del Norte. The length of the town
on the creek may be estimated at one mile, and it is
but three streets in width. Its appearance from a
distance struck my mind with the same effect as a
fleet of flat-bottomed boats such as are seen in the
spring and fall season descending the Ohio River.[18]

In a very detailed account of the commercial conditions,
he states that New Mexico carried on trade directly with
Mexico and "Biscay" as well as with Sonora and Sinaloa.
The exports consisted of sheep, tobacco, dressed skins, fur,
buffalo robes, salt and wrought copper vessels. In exchange
it imported from "Biscay" and Mexico, dry goods, confec-
tionery, arms, iron, steel, ammunition and European wines
and liquors; and from Sonora and Sinaloa, gold, silver and
cheese. The journey from Santa Fé to Mexico and return
was said to take five months.

Although manufacturing was carried on to a reasonable
extent, it was almost entirely in the hands of the Indians,

---

17. Pike, Z. M., *Exploratory Travels* (Rees Ed.), 249.
18. *Ibid.*, 265.

since the Spaniards preferred to give their time to agriculture. He states: "Cultivation is carried on at this place in as great perfection as at any I visited in the province. . . . At this place were as finely cultivated fields of wheat and other small grain as I ever saw, also numerous vineyards."[19]

He describes the people as the bravest and most hardy subjects of New Spain. He attributes this virility to the frontier condition of the district. Their lack of gold and silver he considers as a cause of their remarkable laboriousness. He was much impressed by their hospitality and generosity.[20]

The first to make use of this definite information concerning the conditions in the Spanish province were Robert McKnight, Benjamin Shrive, James Baird and some few others, all citizens of the United States who, in 1812, went up the Missouri River and thence toward the land of opportunity.[21] Following the directions of Pike, they reached Santa Fé in safety. They had evidently believed that the declaration of Mexican independence by Hidalgo, in 1810, had removed the necessity of obtaining passports from the Spanish government. They had not heard of the suppression of the premature uprising, nor did they know that all foreigners, but particularly Americans, were now regarded with increased suspicion. Immediately on their arrival, they were seized as spies; their goods were confiscated; and they were conducted to Chihuahua, where they were imprisoned. They remained prisoners until the final success of the cause of independence under Iturbide, in 1821. They were then released, and some of them made their way back to the United States.[22]

---

19. Bareiro writing in 1832 states that agriculture was almost entirely neglected in his day. (*Ojeada de Sobre Nuevo Mexico*, 23). It is difficult to reconcile those two statements.

20. Pike, Z. M., *Exploratory Travels* (Rees Ed.), 344.

21. *American State Papers*, XII, 435. The original document declaring the entrance of these ten foreigners in 1812 and their imprisonment in accordance with the law forbidding trade by strangers, together with an invoice of their goods is in the Ritch Papers in the Huntington Library (Ritch I, 69).

22. Gregg, J., *Commerce of the Prairies*, I, 19-21. The reports of these men, on their return to their homes, far from discouraging further attempts at carrying

How fixed was the determination to gain access to New
Mexico is evidenced by the report given by Choteau and De
Mun of their attempt in 1817.[23]   They state that while trading upon the Arkansas under a regular license from the
Governor of Missouri, they were forcibly seized and taken
as prisoners to Santa Fé where, after mock trials and an
imprisonment of six weeks and deprivation of their goods,
they were finally released and allowed to find their way home
as best they could.   In demanding damages, they declared
that their loss in merchandise amounted to more than
$30,000.[24]   Their claims were presented by our minister,
Poinsett, to the Mexican authorities.[25]

*Establishment of Regular Trade Between Missouri and
Santa Fé.* The collapse of Spanish power in Mexico, 1821,
made possible a phenomenal increase in the trade which had
been carried on under such unfavorable circumstances when
at least spasmodic efforts were made to enforce the restric-
tive commercial regulations of Spain.   During the first years
in which Mexico, in her inexperience, was attempting the
difficult art of self-government, civil dissension and other
internal difficulties prevented insistence upon the former
restrictions, although they were not formally revoked.   The
news of the increase of intercourse with foreigners upon the
frontier was, however, far from welcome to the Mexican
officials.[26]

Among the many who took advantage of the changed
conditions were Captain William Becknell and four companions, residents of Franklin, Missouri, which had gradually
displaced St. Louis as the frontier commercial post.   They

23. *Senate Document 400*, 24 Congress, 1 Sess., *Passim.*
24. *American State Papers*, XII, 435-452.
25. *Senate Doc. 400*, 24 Congress, 1 Sess.
26. Manning, W. R., *Early Diplomatic Relations between the United States and Mexico*, 166-167.

on trade, induced others to try their fortune therein. The most noted of these
enterprises was led by an Ohio merchant named Glenn, who, after many hardships
finally succeeded, before the close of 1821, in reaching Santa Fé. Jacob Fowler, the
second in command, was the interesting chronicler of the events of this trip. His
journal was edited in a form as nearly as possible approximating the original by
E. Coues, in 1898.

went out in 1821 to trade with the Indian tribes, and eventually made their way to New Mexico where they sold their small cargo at great profit.[27]   The success of these adventurers led Stephen Cooper Walker, and a company of thirty-one men to repeat the trial in 1823.   After untold suffering from lack of water, they finally reached their goal where they, too, advantageously disposed of their goods.[28]

A second enterprise under Becknell in the same year (1822) may be said to mark the beginning of the regular Santa Fé trade.   Chittenden remarks:

> This journey is of historic importance in that it was the first which led directly to San Miguel by way of the Cimarron River instead of following the Arkansas to the mountains; and it was also the first that made use of wagons in the Santa Fé trade.   To William Becknell, therefore, belongs the credit of having made the first regular trading expedition from the Missouri to Santa Fé; of being the first to follow the route direct to San Miguel instead of by way of Taos, and the first to introduce the use of wagons in the trade.[29]

In 1824 wagons began to be employed regularly in place of pack animals, and a well organized company was established at Franklin, Missouri.   The commerce, however, was never monopolized by large companies such as were formed for more northern trade.   That it had grown to remarkable proportions is evidenced by the size of the yearly caravans and the amount of goods transported.   Augustus Storrs, named United States Consul at Santa Fé in 1825, who wrote on New Mexico for Senator Benton, stated that the proceeds for the year 1824 would certainly exceed $180,000.   The round trip was accomplished at this early date in about four months.[30]

---

27. Gregg, J., *Commerce of the Prairies*, I., 21.
28. *Narrative of Adventure of Joel P. Walker*, (Ms. in Bancroft Library).
29. Chittenden, H. M., *The History of the American Fur Trade of the Far West*, II, 503. A document in the Ritch Collection (R. I., 80) Oct. 24, 1824 gives evidence of the friendly relations established between Becknell and the government officials.
30. *Senate Doc. 7, 18 Cong., 2 Sess.*, cited in Niles, 312; Twitchell, R. E., *Leading Facts of New Mexican History*, II, 107.

Opposition of Mexico. The progress being made was not ignored by Mexico. In 1823 Torrens, the Mexican Charge at Washington, reported to his government that an expedition, which seemed to have for its purpose the opening up of a mine as well as the exchange of merchandise, was about to set out from Kentucky for Santa Fé. He suggested that orders be given to prohibit or regulate this traffic, since, otherwise, others would follow the example and end by introducing contraband trade.[31] It was later determined that the mine referred to was within the limits of the United States. But the attitude of the Mexican government was shown by the order to the political chief of New Mexico. He was advised that both the working of the mine and the trade were contrary to the law, and was instructed to enforce the regulations concerning the matter and to prevent the establishment of foreigners there until the final passage of the colonization law, which would formulate rules for their admission.[32] The trade was, however, far too profitable to the residents and officials of New Mexico to be prohibited in accordance with the commands of an ineffective distant government. Therefore traders were rarely inconvenienced by anything more than a high duty, which they could easily afford to pay because of the prices which their goods brought. Their practical monopoly of trade [33] was a necessary outcome of the distance of New Mexico from Mexican ports of entrance or depots of exchange such as Vera Cruz or Mexico City.

Official Provision for a Caravan Road. Owing to the widespread rumors of the importance of the trade between Missouri and Santa Fé, Senator Thomas Hart Benton peti-

31. *La Diplomacia Mexicana*, II, 13-14.· Torrens to Secretario de Relaciones Exteriores.

32. *Ibid.*, 17, 21. On April 20, 1825 instructions were sent to the custom house officials of Taos in regard to the procedure to be followed when traders reached this northern outpoast. There seems to have been no hostile intent in the regulations, but care was to be taken to prevent any attempt to smuggle in contraband goods or sell without a license. (*Ms.* in Archives of New Mexico, folio 75.)

33. An incomplete record (Ritch Papers, I, 81) compiled in Santa Fé in 1825 names fifty-two Americans who were then engaged in trade there.

tioned the Senate of the United States, in December, 1824, on behalf of the inhabitants of Missouri, that facilities be given by the United States "to draw from the bosom of the wilderness an immense wealth which now must be left to grow and perish where it grows, or be gathered by the citizens of some other government to the great loss of Missouri."[34]   Mr. Benton spoke of the value of the trade, not only because of the articles carried out, but because of the silver, fur, and mules which it brought back.   Protection for this trade was sought "and in the form which the character of the trade required—a right of way through the countries of the tribes between Missouri and New Mexico, a road marked out, and security in traveling it, stipulations for good behavior from the Indians and a consular establishment in the provinces to be traded with."[35]   After slight discussion the bill was passed.   This authorized the President to appoint commissioners to mark out a road from the western frontier of Missouri to the boundary line of the United States in the direction of Santa Fé.   It was provided that the consent of the intervening tribes to the marking of the line be obtained, as well as their promise not to molest the citizens of the United States or of Mexico traveling thereon; and that upon the mutual arrangements between the United States and Mexico, the road would be continued to the boundaries of New Mexico.   Ten thousand dollars were appropriated for the marking of the road and $20,000 to defray the expenses of dealing with the Indians.[36]

These measures were carefully noted by Obregon, the minister from Mexico, who in his official report of March 30, 1825, stated that much attention was being given to the commerce from Missouri and that consuls had been appointed to go to Santa Fé, Chihuahua, and Saltillo to protect the interests of the traders.   Since no salaries were affixed to these positions, and the incumbents were to be allowed to

34. *Nile's Register*, XXVI, 253. What other government he referred to, Benton did not state.
35. Benton, T. H., *Thirty Years' View*, II, 41-44.
36. *Register of Debates, 18 Cong.*, 2 Sess., *Appendix*, 102.

engage in trade, it seemed almost certain, he said, that they would resort to illegal commerce. He suggested that a Mexican consul be established at St. Louis to watch the trade and prevent the violation of the recently formed colonization laws.[37] These suggestions were acted upon, and the Mexican government approved the establishment of a consul at St. Louis.

As a result, doubtless, of the warning given by Obregon, the government requested of the governor of Chihuahua a report in regard to the northeastern frontier. In a reply, dated May 13, 1825, Governor Urguidi gave a lengthy description of the region, but remarked that the Anglo-Americans knew the true character of the country better than his own countrymen did. He stated that encouragement was being given by the United States government to settlement therein, and that the effort to open commerce with Mexico was merely a means by which such settlements might be fostered. Because of the low price at which the foreigners could afford to sell their goods, since the former commercial restrictions were relaxed, they were welcomed by the New Mexicans. He suggested that an effort be made to preserve harmony with the United States, but that no advantages be granted which would interfere with the interests of Mexico. His recommendation that the military forces be increased for the purpose of protecting the frontiers and thus fostering colonization by Mexico on the Mexican side, was acted upon, and troops were ordered to Chihuahua and New Mexico.

In 1825, Poinsett, our first minister to Mexico, presented his credentials to the Mexican government. His instructions of prime importance had been in regard to the establishment of a treaty of commerce and of boundaries. A copy of the Act of Congress providing for the road to Santa Fé had been given to him and he was commissioned

---

37. The account herein of the diplomatic relations in regard to the Santa Fé trade is based almost wholly on the able treatment of this subject by W. R. Manning in *Early Diplomatic Relations between the United States and Mexico*, 166-189. He cites as his authority, manuscripts in the *Archivo de Relaciones Exteriores*, Mexico, copies of which are in the Bolton Collection ; and documents in the Dept. of State, Washington, D. C., together with other manuscripts of undoubted authenticity.

to explain that the purpose and spirit actuating the United States in this matter were friendly, and merely an attempt to develop commerce between the two countries. It was assumed that Mexico would lend her assistance to the project by bearing the expense of the construction of the road within Mexican territory.

One month after Poinsett presented his note in regard to this matter, a reply was received from Alaman stating that the question referred to could scarcely be considered apart from the more important general matter of boundaries and commerce. He gave assurance, however, that the Mexican government was convinced that the road would be advantageous to both countries, and would do its part to make the plan a success after the main questions had been disposed of.

Further efforts to hasten the settlement of the joint enterprise were unavailing, and Poinsett remained silent on the matter for a few months.

Although the central government thus failed to give any active support to the movement which seemed to jeopardize its hold on the northern frontier, the officials of New Mexico considered it of vital interest. In 1825, Escudero, a member of the legislature of the state of Chihuahua, traveling from Chihuahua to the United States, passed through Santa Fé. Here, Baca, the political chief of New Mexico, authorized him to negotiate with the United States some means of checking robberies and murders by Indians along the border. On reaching St. Louis he addressed himself to William Clark, the Superintendent of Indian affairs. The latter expressed the desire of the United States to see order established on the border but stated that he had no authority to treat with Escudero. Although Escudero attempted to negotiate with Washington, nothing definite resulted save a demand on the part of Mexico for an explanation of such an assumption of power by an inferior.

In the meantime, the commissioners appointed to mark the road began their work on June 17, 1825 at Fort Osage

on the Missouri River. By September 11, it was completed
to the Arkansas, a distance of four hundred and sixteen
miles. At the Mexican boundary the surveyors, according
to instructions, awaited authorization from Mexico to continue the work. It was hoped that final arrangements with
Mexico would have been completed by the time they reached
that point; but since no instructions were received there,
most of the party returned to Missouri, while Sibley, who
was in charge, and a few others went on to Santa Fé. From
there Sibley wrote to Poinsett, explaining what had been
accomplished; showed at what slight expense and with
what ease the road could be completed and of what advantage it would be to the traders of both nations.

After considerable correspondence between Poinsett
and the Mexican Secretary of Foreign Relations, the Governor of New Mexico, Narbona, was authorized, May 13,
1826, to permit Sibley to continue his task of surveying the
western end of the road. But the work was to be limited
to the survey alone. No trees were to be cut down or marks
erected along the route. Notwithstanding the restrictions,
which were faithfully observed, the road was surveyed from
Santa Fé to connect with the terminal of the road marked
the previous year. "It struck the Arkansas near Plum
Buttes and followed it up to Chouteau Island; thence south
to the Cimarron eighty-seven miles; thence to Rabbit Ear
Creek, and continuing westward entered the mountains
near the source of the Ocate River terminating at Taos."[38]

Little use was made of the road by the traders, however, who preferred to run the risk of possible death from
thirst or Indian attacks on the old and shorter route than
to travel with security on the new but longer one.

---

38. Bancroft, H. H., *Arizona and New Mexico*, 334; *Eighteenth Biennial Report
of Board of Directors of the Kansas State Historical Society*, 107-125. The field notes
of Joseph G. Brown, the engineer of the expedition give a detailed description of
the road surveyed. Here it is made clear that the terminus was San Fernando de
Taos. This record was published for the first time in 1913 by the Kansas State Historical Society. See also Ritch I, 90 and R. I., 91 for incidents connected with the
survey.

Intercourse With California and Chihuahua. The Missouri-Santa Fé trade accelerated the movement of the authorities of New Mexico toward California. In 1829-30 an expedition for the purpose of obtaining the fine mules of California for use in the trade was led by Antonio Armijo. At practically the same time a similar enterprise was undertaken by Ewing Young of Tennessee. Thus was begun a profitable trade between New Mexico and California. The caravans exchanged the woolen fabrics of New Mexico for mules, as well as for silk and other Chinese goods. A profitable trade was likewise developed with Chihuahua and other southern points.[39]

In the trade with Santa Fé the Americans had practically no competitors. This was not true in Chihuahua. Manuel Alvarez, United States Consul at Santa Fé, in a communication to Congress endeavored to obtain privileges which would enable the overland traders to undersell their rivals. In 1842 he wrote:

> The undersigned would represent to Your Honorable bodies that when in the year 1822, the inland trade between Missouri and Santa Fé commenced, it was merely an experiment by some three or four enterprising individuals, who with a few pack animals and a small amount of American goods, sought to open a new market in that quarter.
>
> The success of the first adventurers induced others of more extended means to embark in the trade which continued steadily for several years to augment in magnitude and importance, till eventually a heavy amount of capital was invested in it; great quantities of goods were exported from Missouri into Santa Fé, and thence forwarded to Chihuahua capital of the state of that name.
>
> In the course of time it was ascertained by the western merchants that although they could profitably dispose of the American cotton goods, yet in regard to those of English or French manufacture

---

39. Warner, J. J., *Jedediah Smith and Early California Trappers;* "Itineraire du Nord-Mexico a la Haute Californie parcourie en 1829 et 1830 par soixante Mexicains" in *Bulletin de la Societe de Geographie,* 1835.

they were unable to compete either with the coast merchants who imported such articles directly from their respective countries, or those who brought to the various Mexican sea ports the same class of goods from the United States with the benefit of the debenture laws. Both these parties were enabled in consequence of the less cost of introducing such goods, to undersell and thus drive out of the market those brought by the overland traders from Missouri.

Now the experience of several years has demonstrated, that to send to the market of Chihuahua American goods alone would be to court inevitable loss, both by reason of their bulk and the heavy import duties levied on such goods by the Mexican Government.

To this circumstance in the first place we ascribe the recent rapid declension of the inland trade between Chihuahua and Missouri through Santa Fé, and to the same conjointly with other causes (a statement of which has been submitted to the Executive of the United States) we also attribute the present almost total extinction of the American commerce with Santa Fé itself, in consequence of which the wealthiest and most influential merchants are fast withdrawing from the field.

Repeated applications have been made to Congress at intervals during the last ten years, soliciting that the foreign goods transported in their original packages overland to Santa Fé by our merchants, might enjoy the benefit of debenture, which would place them on an equal footing with those carrying on the trade by sea; but hitherto the applications have been wholly unsuccessful.

The undersigned feeling deeply interested in the prosperity of a traffic, which conjointly with the American residents engaged in it, he has followed and promoted for the last eighteen years, begs leave respectfully to offer for your consideration, the following, as some of the advantages that would result to American interests should the request for our enjoyment of Drawback upon the goods referred to be granted by Congress.

In the first place the inhabitants of the West and particularly those of Missouri by the convenience of a comparatively secure natural road through one of the healthiest regions in the world namely the prairie between Independence and Santa Fé, would command nearly the whole of that portion of the commerce with Chihuahua, which is at present enjoyed by France and England through the seaports of Mexico.

Secondly, within a short time, the whole trade in foreign articles by the State of Chihuahua with the larger portion of that of Durango and Sonora, would be diverted from its present channels and carried on with the United States through Santa Fé; a circumstance which could not fail of producing the most beneficial results to the inhabitants of the West.

The undersigned would state that he has ascertained from the most satisfactory sources that the quantity of foreign goods consumed annually in the State of Chihuahua alone, amounts already to more than $2,000,000 and the demand is steadily increasing. All the profits on so large an amount, now received by foreigners, will, if the desired equality of footing be granted to the inland traders, soon find its way into the hands of the enterprising population of our Western Borders.

Thirdly, it is evident that not only those immediately engaged in the transportation of such goods would be benefited by such a course, but by the increased demand for American goods that would naturally follow, all classes in the Union would participate in their advantages; from the manufacturing districts to the last place in West Missouri where the outfits of the caravans are completed.

Fourthly, it cannot be doubted that a more extensive intercourse between the inhabitants of Missouri and those of the neighboring states of Santa Fé and Chihuahua, would tend greatly to strengthen those feelings of mutual amity and confidence which from their relative geographical position and the intimate connection of their interests it is for the welfare of all parties to cultivate.

Another advantage that would accrue from the more frequent travelling of our Caravans to and fro over the plains inhabited by huge tribes of roving and warlike Indians would be the rendering these familiar with and friendly to the white man and thereby paving the way for and greatly facilitating any operations which the Government of the United States might hereafter have occasion to carry on in that region.

Submitting the preceding suggestions, the undersigned in behalf of the American merchants who have solicited him to represent their situation to Congress, respectfully petitions the Honorable Senate and House of Representatives to take into consideration the expediency of granting them the same privileges of Debenture upon foreign goods exported overland from Missouri to Santa Fé in their original packages, which are enjoyed by those who reship similar goods at the sea ports of the U. S. for exportation to those of Mexico.[40]

The Fur Traders. While the merchants were making their fortunes and acquainting the people of New Mexico with their neighbors on the east, other no less adventurous spirits were penetrating into the remotest corners of the region in their search for fur-bearing animals, particularly the beaver. Their work is not generally so well known as is that of the caravan traders. They have left us few authentic records, for they were well aware of the contraband nature of their work.[41] Among those best known in this field are Ceran St. Vrain, the Patties and Robidoux, although some of the other well known caravan merchants also engaged in fur-trading.

In 1826, Narbona issued a passport to S. W. Williams and Seran Sambrano [42] and thirty-five men with their serv-

---

40. Manuel Alvarez to Senate and House of Representatives, February 1842. (B. M. Read Collection). Although this communication evidently exaggerates the falling off of trade in the later years it gives a good idea of the activities and influence of the leading merchants. The petition was not granted.

41. This account of the fur traders is based on an article in *The Pacific Ocean in History,* "St. Vrain's Expedition to the Gila in 1826," 429-438, by T. M. Marshall, who consulted the written reports of Mexican officials, transcripts of which are in the Bolton Collection.

42. Ceran St. Vrain, (Marshall).

ants, to pass to Sonora for private trade. The party probably numbered one hundred in all. At Santa Fé, or more probably at Taos, the expedition was divided into four parts for convenience in trapping on the various streams.

An amusing complaint was evoked by this influx of Americans. It will be recalled that a certain James Baird, with several companions, had attempted, about 1812, to develop intercourse between Missouri and Santa Fé and gained a prison home for nine years for their efforts.[43] Baird, on his release, evidently became a Mexican citizen engaged in the fur trade. His zeal for his adopted country and incidentally for his own business interests is truly remarkable. In 1826, he wrote the following protest:

> For fourteen years I have resided in the provinces, wherein, according to the Plan of Yguala, I entered upon the enjoyment of the rights of Mexican citizenship, devoting myself for some time to beaver hunting, in which occupation I invested my small means with the purpose of forming a methodical expedition which might bring profit to me and to those fellow citizens, who would necessarily accompany me in the said expedition. I was moved to this project by the protection offered by the laws to Mexican citizens in the employment of their faculties to their own advantage and which excluded by special decrees all foreigners from trapping and hunting, which they might undertake in the rivers and woods of the federation, especially that of beaver, since it is the most precious product which this territory produces. And although it is known to me that for a year and a half past, they have clandestinely extracted a large quantity of peltry exceeding $100,000 in value, I have kept still, knowing that this exploration had been made by small parties; but now, being ready to set out upon the expedition of which I have just spoken, I have learned that with scandal and contempt for the Mexican nation a hundred-off Anglo-Americans have introduced themselves in a body to hunt beaver in the possessions of this state

---

43. See p. 8.

and that of Sonora to which the Rio Gila belongs, and with such arrogance and haughtiness that they have openly said that in spite of the Mexicans they will hunt beaver wherever they please; to protect their expedition, they are carrying powder and balls, in consequence of which no one is able to restrain them. In view of these circumstances, I believe that it is a bounden duty of every citizen, who has the honor to belong to the great Mexican nation, to make known to his superior government the extraordinary conduct which the foreigners observe in our possessions, which transgressions may be harmful, both on account of the insult which they cast upon the nation by despising our laws and decrees as well as through the damage which they do the said nation by the extinction which inevitably will follow of a product so useful and so valuable. I ought to protest, as I do, that in making this report, I am not moved so much by personal interest as by the honor and general welfare of the nation to which I have heartily joined. In view of the foregoing, I beg that Your Excellency may make such provisions as you may deem proper, to the end that the national laws may be respected and that foreigners may be confined to the limits which the same laws permit them and that we Mexicans may peacefully profit by the goods with which the merciful God has been pleased to enrich our soil. . . .[44]

Immediate investigations were ordered, but even before Baird had made his complaint, Narbona had become anxious about the permits which he had granted and tried to make it appear to his home government that he had granted passports, not trading privileges. He was alarmed at the number of foreigners in the country and wrote to the governor of Chihuahua that his forces were inadequate to patrol the frontier.

A report from Don Rafael Sarracino, who had been in New Mexico in 1827, gives us a clear idea of the extent to

---

44. *Archivo de Governacion* (Mexico), *Comercio Expediente*, 44, in Bolton Collection. Cited by Marshall, *op. cit.*, 434-5.

which this sort of enterprise had developed. He wrote:

> The Anglo-Americans, well provided with arms and instruments for hunting, particularly for beaver, are purchasing of the inhabitants of Santa Fé the license which they, in their name, obtain from the judge of that capital, for making a hunt for a certain length of time and in certain places, which the same judge designates for many leagues distance in the mountains and deserts which the Rio Bravo (Rio Grande) washes; with the subterfuge of the license, the Anglo-Americans are attacking the species without limit or consideration and are getting alarming quantities, frequently without paying even an eighth of the customs to the treasury.[45]

In April, 1827, the Mexican Secretary of State for Foreign Relations entered a protest with Poinsett against the conduct of the traders who were violating the commercial laws. Poinsett expressed regret and promised that he would submit the request for redress of grievance to Washington.[46]

Government Protection of the Merchants. Although the caravan trade increased enormously during the next years, there were frequent Indian attacks on small bands of traders. This led to a renewal of demand for government protection. This was granted, and Major Riley was ordered to escort the caravan of June 1829 to the Arkansas with

---

45. Ygnacio Madrid to the Secretary of State and Foreign Relations, April 14, 1831, *Archivo de la Secretario de Governacion* (Mexico), *Jefes Politicos*, p. 1831-1833. *Expedientes*, I, Leg. 59, ff. 28, in Bolton Collection as cited by Marshall, 437. "The Alcalde succeeded in getting twenty-nine tercios (tierces) of very valuable beaver skins which were forfeited in the course of that summer in the storehouses of the deputy commissioner of the territory . . ."

46. Marshall states that he found no evidence to show that the United States took any action to restrain the traders. On the contrary, in July, 1827, William Clark granted permission to thirty-two men to pass through the Indian country to Mexico (Ms. in Huntington Library, Ritch, I, 95). Eighty-four foreigners were reported to have come into New Mexico in July 1827 (Ritch I, 96) and nineteen others passed through Taos in November of the same year. (Ritch, I, 97). An examination of the records kept by the officials of the foreigners in New Mexico proves beyond a doubt the watchfulness of the government in this matter. These records are to be found in the Archives of New Mexico, the files of the Historical Society of New Mexico, and in the Ritch Collection in the Huntington Library.

four companies from Fort Leavenworth. Since it was found
that the most dangerous part of the journey lay just beyond
the Arkansas, the boundary between the United States and
Mexico, Riley and his troops accompanied the traders a
short distance within Mexican territory. The troops remained at Chouteau Island until October 13, when they took
the place of the New Mexican troops who were escorting
to that point the caravan returning from Santa Fé.[47] In
1831, Butler, who had replaced Poinsett as our minister to
Mexico, was instructed by Van Buren, Secretary of State,
to use his influence to have Mexico officially co-operate in the
military protection of the trade. The fact that the treaty
of commerce was considered by Mexico as inseparably
united with the treaty of limits then under consideration,
delayed the final ratification until 1832.[48]

The 32nd article of the Treaty of Commerce, as finally
agreed upon was as follows:

> For the purpose of regulating the interior
> commerce between the frontier territories of both
> Republics, it is agreed that the executive of each
> shall have power, by mutual agreements, of de-
> termining on the route and establishing the roads
> by which such commerce shall be conducted; and in
> all cases where the caravans employed in such com-
> merce shall be conducted; and in all cases where
> the caravans employed in such commerce may re-
> quire convoy and protection by military escort, the
> supreme Executive of each nation, shall, by mutual
> agreement, in like manner, fix on the period of
> departure of such caravans, and the point at which
> the military escort of the two nations shall be
> exchanged. And it is further agreed that until the
> regulations for governing this interior commerce
> between the two nations shall be established that
> the commercial intercourse between the state of
> Missouri, of the United States, and New Mexico in
> the United Mexican States shall be conducted as

---

47. *American State Papers, Military Affairs*, IV, 277-280.
48. The lengthy correspondence in regard to this question is given in the *Register of Debates*, XIV, App. 136-142.

heretofore, each government affording the necessary protection to the citizens of the other.[49]

The report that assistance was being given to the trade
aroused much criticism in the United States on the part of
those who felt that the federal government was overstepping
its authority and showing favoritism to one branch of industry.[50] Because of this opposition, similar military protection was not afforded the next year by the government;
and was only repeated on special occasions, as in 1834, when
Captain Wharton's dragoons were detailed for the service,
and in 1843 when a formidable army under Captain Cooke
escorted two large caravans past the principal points of
danger.[51]

Prohibitive Decree of Santa Ana: Its Repeal. Indian
attacks were checked by the treaties with the tribes. But
on the other hand, bandits from Texas were making frequent raids upon the traders, especially the New Mexicans,
who by this time, were engaged in the commerce in large
numbers. These attacks aroused in Mexico, as well as New
Mexico, violent opposition to the citizens of the United
States. Nor was this animosity allayed by proof being
shown that the perpetrators of the outrages were in no way
subject to the laws of the United States, and, at times,
attacked Americans as well as Mexicans; and that United
States soldiers were employed in efforts to capture them.
It was definitely ascertained that Americans continued to
enter New Mexico without passports and were bringing
firearms to the Indians.[52] In 1840, the Governor, Armijo,
reported to his government that those who accompanied the
annual caravan came for the purpose of spying. He
asserted that they would be justified in reporting that no

---

49. *Tratado de Amistad, Comercio y Navegacion entre los Estados Mexicanos y
los Estados Unidos de America.*
50. *Niles' Register*, XXXVII, 274.
51. Documents in the Archives of New Mexico reveal the frequency of Indian
attacks on the frontier settlements of New Mexico during these years.
52. Armijo to Minister of War, 1837. In the Bolton Transcripts.

effective opposition could be offered to any foreign attack since the military force was ridiculously small.[53]

Although the organized attempt of Texas to gain the allegiance of the New Mexicans was a dismal failure,[54] it had a baneful effect on the commerce between the United States and New Mexico as well as on the treatment accorded to Americans residing in New Mexico. The following letter addressed to the Secretary of State, Daniel Webster, reveals the degree of hostility developed.

Sir

In a moment of extreme excitement and danger *We* a few isolated American citizens together with a few others, citizens of other nations, feel it our duty to apprise the Government of the United States of the circumstances by which we are surrounded and oppressed here at this moment.

It has been ascertained here that an invading expedition of about three hundred and twenty-five men from Texas is approaching this territory; the inhabitants of which in unison with the principle officers of the Government have become so exasperated against all the foreigners here that we consider our lives and properties in imminent danger; and it is our fear that long ere this shall have reached Washington we shall all have been robbed and probably murdered.

This morning the Governor left here with his troops for the purpose of repelling those invaders; immediately after he left the principle plaza or square of the town one of his officers (apparently to us his principle and next in command to himself who is also his nephew and confidant) returned rode up to the door of Mr. Manuel Alvarez Consul of the United States at this place; and with the assistance of several of his soldiers and a crowd of the populace entered the house of the Consul, whom they grossly insulted personally abused and wounded in the face, however on the interposition of some of the better disposed of the Mexican citizens the riot was appeased; but previous to this

---

53.   *Ibid.*, Feb. 4, 1840.
54.   See below, Chapter VII.

. . . he stated in the publick street and in the hearing of a large multitude of the Citizens that after having vanquished these Texians he would return and destroy all us foreigners.

This conduct together with innumerable insults injustices and unlawful oppressions, to which we are daily subjected proves clearly to us the inveterate feeling that this Governor with many of his citizens have towards us.

Had there ever occurred any dispute between this officer and our Consul we might have supposed that this attack was made on the latter to gratify personal revenge, but as nothing of this kind had ever occurred we are forced to the conclusion that it was only the outbreaking in one person of the evil spirit which exists in the bosoms of the Principle authorities, and also in those of a large majority of the citizens towards us foreigners who are here.

We therefore hope that by making this circumstance known to our Government it will adopt of such measures as will prevent a reccurrence of such injuries to its citizens.[55]

Thus was generated much ill feeling, and the relations between the Americans and authorities of New Mexico were becoming more and more strained until, finally, President Santa Ana closed the Northern ports to foreign commerce and imposed restrictions on all retail trade by a decree signed at his palace of Tacubaya, August 7, 1843.[56]

On January 25, 1844, Almonte reported to the Mexican Government that, according to an article in the *National Intelligencer*, there was great discontent in Santa Fé on account of the closing of the ports; and that there was reason to fear that this might encourage the sentiment in favor of annexation to Texas. He suggested that the traffic be regulated rather than prohibited.[57] So great was the opposition to the proposed forcible termination of the

---

55. To Daniel Webster, Secretary of State, Sept. 16, 1841. Signed by thirteen American residents in Santa Fe. (Doc. in B. M. Read Collection.)

56. Gregg, J., *Commerce of the Prairies*, II, 177; *Ho. Ex. Doc. 2*, 28 Cong. 1 Sess.

57. *Almonte to Ministro de Relaciones Exteriores y Gobernacion*, January 25, 1844. In Bolton Collection.

traffic, that the decree was repealed on March 31, 1844, almost before it had gone into effect. Although the selling price had decreased, and, therefore, the profits lessened, the trade of the next years was as great as ever.[58]

From its inception the Santa Fe trade had been of great value to Missouri. Young men, of whose numbers we can only conjecture since no two accounts agree, sought fortune and opportunity in the apparently high remunerative business. There can be no doubt about the influence this widely known trade had in filling out the new frontier. Fearing that the commerce would be deflected from the original points of departure, attempts were made to minimize the value of the profits in the reports which appeared in the press.

As early as 1824, a resident of Franklin, Missouri, did his part to keep the trade in the hands of those then engaged therein. He reported: "This trade is done, as all will inform you." The editor of the paper, *The Missouri Intelligencer*, in which this appeared, when called to task for allowing such a contribution to be published replied:

> Our own citizens were the first to explore the route and find the market, and in our opinion, ought to reap the advantages resulting from the discovery. We have generally stated plain matters of fact, in regard to this trade, abstaining from all unnecesary embellishments or exaggeration, which could only have a tendency to attract the attention of other states, and induce large bodies to engage in it, to the injury of our own citizens and to the annihilation of the commerce itself by glutting the market. Already has a large party left Tennessee, and another from Alabama, (the latter taking $80,000 worth of merchandize) and but a few days since, a gentleman from Boston, an agent

58. Bancroft, H. H. *Arizona and New Mexico*, 337. A good account of the trading conditions during the later Mexican period is given in the *Memoirs of James J. Webb* in the papers of the Historical Society of New Mexico. One itemized list of articles brought in by one trader is but a type of dozens of a similar nature to be found in the Archives of New Mexico and the Ritch Collection of the Huntington Library. See Ritch I, 226.

of an extensive commercial concern, passed
through this place on his way to New Mexico, for
the purpose of ascertaining the real situation of
the Market, and if favorable to engage in the business extensively. *That country cannot support the
trade to the extent it is now carried on.* Missouri
alone can supply that country with twice the
amount of goods it has the means to purchase.
Our position enables us to carry on the traffic to
greater advantage than any other state in the
Union.[59]

Of the various articles brought back to Missouri, the
most important was specie. Money was scarce on the frontier to the great detriment of business development. "Opening an avenue to Mexico by which specie can be procured in
exchange for American productions, is, therefore, an object
of much and just importance."[60] Although the Mexican
coinage in circulation had no legal status, Congress interested itself in the question, between 1830 and 1834, and a
number of bills were introduced which had as objects making foreign coin, or at least Mexican silver dollars, legal
tender. In 1834, a law provided that the dollars of the
Spanish-American countries were legal tender "provided
they were of certain fineness and weighed not less than 415
grains (gross weight)."[61] The soundness of the bank of
Missouri is attributed to the backing given it by the Santa
Fé traders for whom it served as a place of deposit on their
return from New Mexico.[62]

It was futile to expect that such success would not
arouse the active interest of those who saw a way to utilize
the trade for their own ends. In February 1845, and again
in March of the same year, Thomas D. Hailes, who claims

59. *Mo. Inte.*, June 18, 1825, as cited in F. F. Stephens, "Missouri and the Santa
Fe Trade" in *The Missouri Historical Review*, XI, 301-2, The excellent articles by this
author which appeared in Vols. X and XI of the *Review* give an exhaustive study of
the influence of the trade on Missouri. For the places of origin of thirty-four foreigners recorded as residing in New Mexico in 1839 see Ritch I, 174.

60. *Ibid.*, 305.
61. *Ibid.*, 307-9.
62. *Ibid.*, 311.

to have been British vice consul at New Orleans for many years, addressing himself to Luis G. Cuevas, the Mexican Minister of Foreign Relations, offered his services as Mexican consul at Independence, Missouri, for the States of Indiana, Illinois and Missouri. He represented that the revenue derived by Mexico from the overland trade was unwarrantably small, due to the fact that there was no Mexican Consular Agent at Independence, the point of departure of the trade, with resulting fraudulence on the part of the traders; and to the custom of imposing a fixed tax on each wagon load without regard to its value. It is easy to believe his statement that: "Dues are, in different ways, evaded, and a vastly lucrative revenue comparatively withheld. You may imagine something of the rest by my instancing the practice of the Traders, of making one load of two, by doubling teams, on the eve of reaching the place of destination." Some of the statements in his communication give an insight into the actual conditions. In suggesting that a definite tax per yard be levied on cloth, he asserts:

> A wagon load of 5,000 pounds (their average weight) is equal to 24,000 square yards, which at five cents would yield a Duty of twelve hundred dollars—being twice the sum now exacted. The trade warrants that rate of Duty, from the fact that the cost in the United States is about 9 to 12½ cents per yard, and sells in Mexico at Durango at 31¼ to 50 cents cash. Calico, I consider, could afford to pay 7 cents per yard Duty, and fine goods of all denominations, 15 per cent, on the value at the place of destination . . . The service of the appointment to watch over the interests of Mexican Trade in that extensive region filled with citizens of enterprising commercial character is obvious.

He estimated the revenue which would accrue to Mexico rather high, for in urging his petition, he declared: ". . . I firmly believe I should experience disappointment did it not produce $50,000 to the Treasury and it would prove a remarkable affair indeed if the issue were not more beneficial."[63] There is no evidence available that this petition was granted. The entire tone of the letter would lead one to doubt the sincerity or trustworthiness of the writer, and the Mexican officials would scarcely appoint a non-Mexican to such an important post as late as 1845 when relations between Mexico and the United States were becoming so strained. Rather, Mexico watched with increasing uneasiness the gradual assumption of power or influence by the foreigners who remained permanently on its soil.

Trapper and trader had beaten out the path between the western American frontier and the northern Mexican outpost, Santa Fé.[64] From its inception at the opening of the nineteenth century, the commercial intercourse between the two regions had steadily gained in magnitude until enormous interests were vested therein. The mistrust bred of lack of mutual understanding had been largely destroyed, but as the Mexican government had feared, the violation of the Spanish trade restrictions greatly facilitated the American military conquest of New Mexico.

63. *Relaciones Exteriores*, Mexico, *D. F. Comercio*, 1825-1849, in *Bolton Collection*.

64. An interesting popular account of the Santa Fé trade and related topics is to be found in Ruffus, R. L., *The Santa Fé Trail*.

CHAPTER II

THE SETTLERS

The American traders were not long content to remain simply as passers-by in this land of opportunity. To many, New Mexico was sufficiently far west to satisfy their desire for "elbow room" and they made it their permanent home. The exclusive Mexican colonial laws which were abrogated only in 1842 by Santa Ana [1] while placing a difficulty in the way of obtaining land grants were not, apparently, an insuperable obstacle.

John Heath. In the absence of complete records, it is impossible to determine whether or not all these adventurous pioneers complied with the letter of the law and swore allegiance to Mexico. There is abundant evidence that many sought and obtained full naturalization.[2] In the second expedition under Becknell was a certain John Heath who as "Juan Gid" received a grant of land at the Bracito as early as 1823.[3] and in 1831, George Pratt and William Hague, non-Mexicans surely, if names are an index, were able to lease land in Santa Fé.[4]

La Junta Tract. Scarcely less valuable was the grant given, in 1845, to Scolly, Gidding, Smith and others, who became Mexican citizens and were thereupon given title to the La Junta Tract, 108,507.64 acres in area, in Mora County. This was soon converted into flourishing farms.[5]

Bent's Fort. Among those who married into the old families were some who later played a prominent part in the history of their adopted country. Pre-eminent among

1. *Spanish Archives of New Mexico,* I, 275.
2. Record of the naturalization papers are to be found principally in the Ritch Collection, Huntington Library. Some are still in the Archives of New Mexico. One document (Ritch I, 113, 1-3) names thirty-nine persons to whom papers were given in 1829-31.
3. *Spanish Archives of New Mexico,* I, 124-5. The Court of Private Land Claims established in 1891 rejected the claim which had increased to 108,000 acres.
4. *Ibid.,* 270. In the Archives of New Mexico, Folio 72, Pratt is called a Frenchman.
5. *The Spanish Archives of New Mexico,* I, 276-8; *New Mexico Blue Book,* 129. John Scolly has the honor of having brought the first modern plows to New Mexico. There are other grants listed in the *Blue Book* which must have been to Americans.

these stands Charles Bent who was named first governor by
Kearny after the conquest.[6] A native of Virginia, after
graduating from West Point he resigned from the army and
engaged in business in St. Louis. In 1828, he set out on the
Santa Fé Trail to look for a favorable place in which to
establish a supply-store for the traders and a depot for the
fur trade. With his brother William, only less famous than
himself, and Ceran St. Vrain, he built the famous Bent's
Fort.[7] These were the first settlers in the vicinity of the
trail in what is now Colorado.[8]

Wislizenus, after a visit to the fort, in 1839, says: "On
Sept. 15th we reached Bent's Fort. It lies on the left bank
of the Arkansas, close by the river, and is the finest and
largest fort which we have seen on this journey . . . The
fort is about one hundred and fifty miles from Taos in
Mexico and about three hundred from Santa Fé. Little expeditions go frequently to the former city to barter for
flour, bread, beans, sugar, etc. Then, too, much merchan-
dize is annually transported by ox teams to this point from
the boundary of Missouri which is only six hundred miles
distant."[9]

It was not only a center for commercial activities but
also the favorite rendezvous for any Americans who hap-
pened to be in the vicinity. It was there they would hear the
latest news from "the States." This assembling of foreigners on the immediate frontier was viewed with apprehension by the officials of New Mexico. In 1840, Governor
Armijo reported:

Many years' experience has shown me that the
dangers from which the Department suffers result
from the various fortresses which North Americans have placed very near this Department, the

6. Letter of introduction of C. Bent by B. Riley of U. S. Army to Governor of
Santa Fé, July 10, 1820.   Ritch I, 331.
7. Twitchell, R. E., Leading Facts of New Mexican History, II, 234.
8. Benton, B., "The Taos Rebellion" in Old Santa Fe, I, 207.
9. Wislizenus, F. A., A Journey to the Rocky Mountains, 141. A restoration of
Bent's Fort is to be seen in the rooms of the Historical Society of New Mexico,
Santa Fé.

nearest of which is that of Charles Bent on the Napestle (Arkansas) River on the farther bank. Be kind enough to acquaint the President that if he does not soon remedy this, New Mexico must go to total ruin. These forts are the protection of contraband trade by their contact with the first populated frontier by this Department, San Fernando de Taos, where the people are familiar with these strangers. These are the very ones who supply arms and ammunition to most of the barbarous tribes. These are the protection of robbers, either foreigners or Mexicans. These are the ones who dispose all the barbarian nations to rob and kill the Mexicans either in this Department or other Departments of the interior in order that they may profit by the spoils.[10]

Meanwhile the Fort was daily increasing in popularity and importance. After great success in the first enterprise, the firm set up a general merchandise business in Santa Fé, which was even more prosperous than the first.[11]

Taos was of more strategic importance to commerce than even Santa Fé. Charles Bent was the most influential person there during many years. His correspondence with Manuel Alvarez, United States Consul at Santa Fé, kept the latter informed of every movement of interest which occurred in the northern outpost. He seems to have made himself responsible for the protection of American lives and property on the frontier and apparently had little respect for legal procedure. In one place he asserts:

"I think the Governor is not a man entirely destitute of honorable feelings he well knows there

10. Armijo to Secretary of War, Feb. 4, 1840, in the *Bolton Transcripts*. Since this was but one of the many communications designed to inspire in the central government some realization of the exposed state in which New Mexico was at the time, and the consequent ease with which a small foreign force could conquer it, one hesitates to accept unquestioningly all the statements of the hostile governor. But there is grave reason to believe that not all those who found hospitality at Bent's Fort would rally to the defense of Mexico in case of invasion.

11. Twitchell, R. E., *op. cit.*, II, 234. The Bent Letters in the Read Collection and the Alvarez Letters in the files of the Historical Society of New Mexico reveal clearly the influence Charles Bent had in New Mexico. His position was doubtless strengthened by his marriage to the prominent Maria Ignacia Jaramillo.

are cases that the satisfaction that the law gives amounts to nothing. I had rather have the satisfaction of whipping a man that has wronged me than to have him punished ten times by the law, the law to me for a personal offence is no satisfaction whatever, but cowardes and women must take this satisfaction. I could possibly have had Vigil araned for trial for slander but what satisfaction would this have bean to me to have had him fined, and moreover I think he has nothing to pay the fine with. . . ."[12]

We are indebted to Charles Bent for the list of American citizens living in Taos in 1841.[13]

John Roland	Maried, naturlised	Distiller & farmer
William Gordon		Gun Smith & farmer
Francis Bedwell		Distiller
Antoine LeRoux	Maried, naturlised	farmer
George Long	Maried	Distiller
Edmon Conn	Carpenter & Distiller	Naturalized
Fredric Batcheler		Cooper
Simeon Turly		Distiller
Manel Le Fever	Maried	Laborer
Stephen L. Lee	Naturlised, Maried	Merchant
W. C. Moon		Cooper
John Reed	Maried	Distiller
James Jeffrey		Laborer
Fredric Loring	Naturlised	Taylor
William Workman	Naturlised	Merchant
Chas. Bobean	Do. maried	Do.
Chas. Bent	———	———
Antoine Le Doux	Maried	Farmer
Abram Le Doux	Maried	Farmer
Raffial Carifil		Hatter
Joseph Begou	Maried	Laborer
Pier Quennell	Maried	Laborer

The Canadians that are heare named are such as ware in the Teritory of Missouri at the time the Transfer was made by France to the United States in the year 1803. They are considered Citizens of the U. S. C. Bent (C. Bent to M. Alvarez, *Ms.* in Historical Society of New Mexico Collection.)

These men were respected by those who became personally acquainted with them. Their services were invaluable to many. One who knew Charles Bent narrates:

---

12. C. Bent to M. Alvarez in *Read Collection.*
13. The following list was sent by C. Bent to Manuel Alvarez on January 30, 1841.

He was a noble man and a great business man—was considered the head of the firm of "Bent and St. Vrain," his influence was considerable in New Mexico. I remember seeing him in Santa Fé on the arrival of Col. Sam Owen's Train of merchandise wagons from Independence Mo. The duties levied by the Mexican Government at that time was $600 on each wagon load of goods, and Col. Sam Owens, owner of ten large wagon loads of goods, put up in Bales, left his train in charge of old Nicholas Gentry, at the crossing of the river on the Cimaron route and with one or two other gentlemen going out to Mexico for a pleasure trip went by way of Fort Bent, and reached Santa Fe long before his train of wagons reached the first settlements of New Mexico, and there he made a settlement with the Customs House Officers and Mexican Authorities, through the influence of Charles Bent getting his ten Wagon loads of merchandise passed at a greatly reduced rate . . . It was said that little of the duties on American Food brought overland into New Mexico ever reached the General Government, on account of the laxity and mode of the officers in Santa Fé. A man of influence like Don Carlos Bent, as he was known by the Mexicans, could do much toward getting the exorbitant duties reduced on American merchandise.[14]

Of perhaps greater fame, if of less influence during the Mexican period, was one to whom Bent's Fort was practically home. This was "Kit" Carson related by marriage to Charles Bent for he married Josefa Jaramillo, the sister of Charles Bent's wife. While the name of Kit Carson means much in the history of the pioneers of New Mexico this region did not claim his entire attention. The whole southwest was familiar to him. He began his career as a trader in 1827. A contemporary describes him thus: "He was naturally a commander. Personally he was mild, rather effeminate voice, but when he spoke, his voice was one that would draw the attention of all . . . His language was forci-

---

14. Boggs, Thos., O., *Ms., Bancroft Library.*

ble, slow, and pointed, using the fewest words possible . . . Everybody admired him . . . He had a special influence over Indians.[15]

The Robidoux Brothers. Antoine and Louis Robidoux of St. Louis were also early identified with the Santa Fé trade. They, too, established their homes in New Mexico, at Taos and at Santa Fe. Antoine married the adopted daughter of Governor Armijo. Sabin writing of the "Dramatis Personae" of the early day in New Mexico thus comments on Antonio Robidoux:

> First fur trader out of old Taos, whose post in southwest Coloradeo was the pioneer American trading post beyond the Continental Divide of the Rockies; later with a post established at the forks of the Uintah River in northeastern Utah, Fort Uintah, captured and destroyed in 1844 by the Utes. One of New Mexico's earliest gold miners— setting the fashion by "sinking eight thousand dollars." Interpreter and guide with the Kearny overland column of 1846 to California, where his brother, Louis Robidoux, who had preceded him by two years was *alcalde* and *juez de paz* at San Bernardino; grievously wounded by a lance thrust at the battle of San Pasqual; granted a pension by Congress May 23, 1856; died at St. Joseph Missouri (former trading post of his second brother, Joseph), in 1860, aged 66. A "thin man" of the French Canadian type, active member of a family along the Missouri, in the Southwest and in California . . .[16]

Joab Houghton. Among the names which stand out prominently in the annals of the first years after the American conquest in 1846, that of Joab Houghton holds an important place. A native of New York State, he went to

---

15. Breevort, E., *The Santa Fe Trail*, (Ms.) 5. So much has been written about "Kit" Carson that it seems unnecessary to go into any further details here. His home and grave today, are tourist attractions in Taos.

16. Sabin, E. L., *Kit Carson Days*, 121. In 1829 the brothers Antoine and Louis sought and obtained naturalization papers. (Ritch I, 111 and 113. See also Ritch I, 116.) Their passport was secured in 1825 from Wm. Clark, Superintendent of Indian affairs. (Ritch I, 83).

New Mexico in 1844,[17] and was appointed United States consul at Santa Fé, in 1845. He engaged in merchandising with a man by the name of Leitensdorfer, and from 1846 to 1848 their mercantile house, established in Santa Fé, had the reputation of being one of the leading west of the Missouri River. Mr. Houghton was named by Kearny as one of the judges of the supreme court established in New Mexico in 1846. His career in this position was not a success. He had been educated as a civil engineer. This, evidently, did not fit him for a judicial position.

Doubtless there were countless others who followed the example of these leaders of men, and to all intents and purposes, identified themselves with the people among whom they chose to dwell.

Beaubien Grant. But among all the enterprising "foreigners" perhaps the most successful was Carlos Beaubien, originally from Canada but who resided in the United States from 1812 to 1823.[18] At the latter date he went to New Mexico and in time became a Mexican citizen. In 1841, he and Guadalupe Miranda, a prominent Mexican, filed a petition for a grant of land partly in Colorado in Las Animas County.

The petition requested a tract of land "commencing below the junction of the Rayado and Red rivers, from thence in a direct line to the east of the first hills, from thence following the course of the Red River in a northerly direction of Una de Gato with Red River; from thence following along said hills to the east of the Una Gato River to the summit of the table land (mesa) from whence, turning northwest, following said summit to the summit of the mountain which separates the waters of the rivers which run towards the east from those which run to the west, from thence following the summit of said mountain in a southerly

17. Ritch I, 223. In the Ms. his name is given as Juan Houghton.
18. Charles Hippolyte Trotier, Sieur de Beaubien was descended from a long line of noble ancestors. The family became well represented in America. Various members became prominent in affairs in this country and in Canada. Upon leaving Canada, Charles used the name Beaubien by which he was thereafter known. (*History of New Mexico*, I, 189).

direction to the first hill east of the Rayado River, from thence following along the brow of said hill to the place of beginning." [19]

In requesting the grant, the petitioners made use of the usual declarations of unselfish and patriotic motives.

An old and true adage says that what is the business of all is the business of none; therefore, while the fertile lands in New Mexico, where without contradiction, nature has proven herself most generous, are not reduced to private property, where it will be improved, it will be of no benefit to the Department . . . The welfare of a nation consists in the possession of lands which produce all the necessaries of life without requiring those of other nations, and it cannot be denied that New Mexico possesses this great advantage, and only requires industrious hands to make it a happy residence . . . Under the above conviction we both request your excellency to be pleased to grant us a tract of land for the purpose of improving it, without injury to any third party, and raising sugar beets, which we believe will grow well and produce an abundant crop, and in time to establish manufactories of cotton and wool and raising stock of every description.

The petition was granted by Governor Armijo the following January. Immediately a claim was filed on the part of the chiefs of the Pueblo of Taos on the ground that the same district had already been given to them by Charles Bent. The title was therefore suspended by the then acting governor, Mariano Chavez.

The assertion of Beaubien and Miranda that the land described by the Taos claimants was not the same as that asked for in the petition "which does not exceed fifteen or eighteen leagues" finally prevailed and in 1844, Armijo, reappointed as governor, referred the question to the departmental assembly which was then in session. The decree of Chavez was reversed.

---

19. Twitchell, *Spanish Archives of New Mexico*, I, 62-3.

At first the vast estate of truly feudal dimensions was operated by Beaubien and Miranda in partnership. Miranda later sold his share to Beaubien, whose son-in-law, Lucien B. Maxwell, made the grant famous. In 1846, when Beaubien and Maxwell first met, the latter was already known far and wide for his lavish hospitality dispensed from his "mansion" on the Cimarron. His wealth consisted in flocks of sheep which throve remarkably in the unnumbered acres over which they roamed unhindered. "At this time the whole region between 'El Pueblo' in Colorado, and Fernando de Taos in New Mexico was almost unknown, certainly unexplored; excepting those portions traversed by the few traders travelling between Santa Fé and the Missouri River. But every trader, every *major domo*, every teamster, every soldier, who passed over this part of the trail knew Maxwell and most of them were known to him by name.[20]

Maxwell's home is described as being as much a palace as the circumstances and times permitted. "Some of its apartments were most sumptuously furnished, after the prevailing Mexican style, while others were devoid of all but table, chairs and cards for poker . . ."[21] Had a guest book been kept, the names of practically all those whose fame had gone abroad in the southwest would have been recorded. "Kit Carson, ex-governor Thomas Boggs, Richens (Uncle Dick) Wooten, Don Jesus Abreu, Colonel Ceran St. Vrain, and other men whose names are well known in the pioneer history of the Santa Fé trail, made his home a rendezvous for years."[22]

Although it was not until 1864, on the death of his father-in-law, that Maxwell purchased the entire grant, he had associated himself so intimately with the veritable principality that it is under his name that the tract, which

20. *History of New Mexico*, 180. (Pacific States Publishing Co.)
21. *Idem.*
22. *Idem.*

ultimately came to embrace 1,714,000 acres, is best known.[23] The success of Beaubien and Miranda was an inspiration to others. In November 1845,[24] "the citizen Gervace Nolan and associates" made a most compelling request for a similar grant from Governor Armijo.

> . . . I have found a piece of land, in the little canon of Red River, vacant, unpopulated, and uncultivated . . . being situated to the south of the possession of Messrs. Miranda and Beaubien, which in the name of our supreme powers of the Mexican nation, we solicit from the benignity of your excellency to be pleased to grant us the favor of giving us the possession of said land, marking out to us, as its boundaries, on the north, the possessions of said Messrs. Miranda and Beaubien; on the south, one league in a direct line, including the Sapello river, according to its current (cordillera) ; on the west, another league from Red river, and its current; and on the southeast, the little hills of Santa Clara, with their range to the little canon of Ocate. It is to be observed that a very small portion of said land is susceptible of cultivation; but what is more important, is to establish the raising of horned cattle, sheep, horses.[25]

In order to prove that the petitioners were worthy of the grant, Nolan asserted that he had resided in the country for twenty-three years; had rendered service, either in campaigns or contributions, whenever called upon.[26] The request met with the approval of Armijo, who ordered the Justice of the Peace of Lo de Mora to put Nolan and his associates in possession.[27] In 1848, two of the original grantees, Juan Antonio Aragon and Antonio Maria Lucero,

---

23. In 1882 the United States filed a bill in chancery in the United States circuit court to cancel the patent. The suit was won by the Maxwell Co. For an account see Twitchell, *The Spanish Archives of New Mexico*, I, 51-65.

24. The document is dated 1825, which is very evidently a mistake.

25. *Ho. Ex. Doc.* 28, 36 Cong. 2 Sess., 8.

26. *Idem.* Nolan was naturalized in 1829 (Ritch I, 113. He was in Taos in 1827. R I, 97.)

27. The name of the Justice of the Peace, Thomas Benito Lalanda, indicates the gradual incorporation of the erstwhile traders in the population. It seems incredible that this does not point to connection with Bapiste La Lande already referred to.

surrendered their claims for an apparently trivial compensation to Nolan. He thus came into possession of an estate which eventually came to include 575,968 acres.[28]

It is not surprising that a great deal of uncertainty existed regarding the legality of many of the grants made so prodigally. There were numerous changes in the Constitution of Mexico as well as in the acts of the Mexican Congress regarding land grants. Frequently such grants were issued by officials who did not have the legal authority to do so. Because of the length of time it necessarily took to inform frontier officials of the changes, these grants, doubtless, were made in perfect good faith, but when investigated could not be maintained. Moreover, these grants to both Mexicans and Americans were expressed in the vaguest terms. For instance, it is said, the assigned length was "from the old sheep corral of Jesus Maria Gonzales up the Creek to Monument rock." The width extended from the bed of the stream to the "faldas" of the mountains on either side. The ambiguity of the word "faldas" justified almost any interpretation.[29]

Although the majority of those who obtained superb estates during the Mexican regime did not succeed in having their claims ratified by the United States, they enjoyed revenue and prestige during the years in which American influence was beginning to make itself felt. Gradually the "Foreigner" was becoming a fellow-countryman. It would

---

28. According to Mexican land laws only Mexican citizens could acquire ownership of land. In filing a request for confirmation of the title in 1860, according to the Act of Congress, 1854, which created the office of surveyor general for New Mexico and ordered the filing of all claims, Wheaton, the attorney for the heirs of Nolan, declared that the latter was a naturalized Mexican citizen but that his naturalization papers were destroyed in a fire in Marysville, California. (*Ibid.*, 16) The total claim was rejected by the Court of Private Land Claims.

29. *History of New Mexico*, I, 208-0. The famous Fossat or Quicksilver Mine Case in California involved a lengthy discussion of the meaning of the word *falda*. The opinion given was that ". . . evidence from poets, other dictionaries, and other prose writers tended to prove that if falda meant skirt, it meant the edge of the skirt its extremity as well as its higher folds." (II Wallace, 649-728).

not be long before he would be the leader in the new country.[30]

College of the Holy Names,
Oakland, California.

---

30. By the Treaty of Guadalupe-Hidalgo, 1848, the United States agreed to recognize land claims which were duly authenticated. "Squatters," however, would see no difference between the already granted New Mexican land and the rest of the public domain. Endless litigation was the result. It was only settled by the tardy establishment of the Court of Private Land Claims, 1891, whose sole duty was to finally adjudicate between the conflicting claims. Numerous reports of the findings of this court are found in the various histories of New Mexico.

CHAPTER III

DIPLOMATIC EFFORTS TO OBTAIN NEW MEXICO

During the years of turmoil following Mexico's declaration of independence from Spain, many complaints were made to their home governments by foreigners residing in the country because of Mexico's inability to protect them and their business interests. For twenty years before the outbreak of the war between the United States and Mexico, the question of the claims of American merchants who demanded restitution for alleged confiscation of property constituted one of the most important points of controversy between the two nations. As in all such cases, there can be no doubt that some of the claims were largely fictitious or highly exaggerated.[1]

The Texas question, on which the leaders of thought in the United States were divided into two hostile camps, ultimately became inextricably bound up with this matter. Any attempt at the adjustment of the various problems involved seemed, to the enemies of the successive administrations, a furtive attempt to obtain possession of western domain which would serve as a stepping-stone to the Pacific and increase slave territory.

Initial Attempt to Acquire Mexican Territory. Foundation for such attacks was found in the instructions to successive ministers to Mexico beginning with Butler in 1829. He was personally instructed by President Jackson to use his utmost endeavors to purchase Texas. This was but a repetition of the instructions which Van Buren, as Secretary of State, had drawn up for Poinsett, the previous minister to

---

1. Kohl, C. C., *Claims as a Cause of the Mexican War* VII, 78; Maning, W. R., *Early Diplomatic Relations between the United States and Mexico*, 252-276.

Mexico, wherein great stress was laid on the advantage which would accrue to Mexico by her cession of a portion of the territory of Texas for a pecuniary consideration; and Mr. Poinsett was urged to spare no effort to have the boundary settled according to instructions, since this alone would insure to the citizens of the United States the undisputed navigation of the Mississippi.[2] This message had not been sent to Poinsett because of his recall.

Butler did not succeed in accomplishing anything, and was recalled in 1835 because of complaints made by Mexico to the United States in regard to his conduct. Powhatan Ellis was appointed to fill his place as *charge d'affaires.* In 1836, Forsyth, Secretary of State, wrote to Ellis:

> The claims of citizens of the United States on the Mexican Government for injuries to their persons or property by the authorities or citizens of that republic are numerous and of considerable amount, and though many of them are of long standing, provision for their payment is pertinaciously withheld, and the justice of most of them has not been acknowledged.[3]

At Ellis' suggestions a more vigorous policy was determined upon. In a dispatch from Mr. Forsyth, the grievances against Mexico were reviewed, and Ellis was instructed to demand his passports if satisfactory investigation and reparation were not undertaken without undue delay. Thus diplomatic relations would be severed.[4] Ellis followed the letter of his instructions and, not receiving a satisfactory reply, demanded his passports, Dec. 13, 1836.[5]

The Gaines-Gorostiza Episode. Matters were also approaching a crisis in the United States, but on wholly different grounds. Texas, having declared her independence of Mexico, was anxiously seeking recognition and annexation by the United States. Her ministers had aroused enthusi-

---

2. *House Ex. Doc.* 42, 25 Cong., 1 Sess., pp. 10-16.
3. *House Ex. Doc.* 351, 25 Cong., 2 Sess., XII, p. 160.
4. *House Ex. Doc.* 105, 25 Cong., 2 Sess., pp. 24-27.
5. *Ibid.* 51.

astic interest among our citizens, although the officials hesitated to take a decisive step.[6]

On January 23, 1836, President Jackson, through Secretary of War, Lewis Cass, instructed General Gaines to advance to the western frontier of Louisiana to prevent Indian depredations and the crossing of the boundary by armed contestants who had already taken or might take part in the conflict between Texas and Mexico. A later note gave instructions not to advance beyond Nacogdoches.[7]

Gorostiza, the Mexican minister to the United States, entered a protest against the order and requested that it be revoked as a violation of neutrality, since there could be no doubt that the region referred to lay within the boundaries of Mexico.[8] In reply, Forsyth represented that since the treaty of limits had not yet been drawn up there could be no definite decision as to where the true boundary lay. He stated:

> . . . The troops of General Gaines will be employed only in protecting the interests of the United States and those of the Mexican territory according to the obligations of the treaty between the two powers. Whether the territory beyond the United States belongs to the Mexican Government or the newly declared Texan State is a question into which the United States does not propose to enter.[9]

A lengthy correspondence was carried on between Gorostiza and Forsyth in which Gorostiza endeavored to have the instructions countermanded and Forsyth held to the view that the authority given to General Gaines was in full accord with former treaties, and that the Mexican official had no reason to fear that an attempt would be made later to base any claims on the occupation of the region; that

---

6. Garrison, "Texan Diplomatic Correspondence," in *Annual Report of the Amer. Hist. Asso.* 1907, vol. 2, *passim; House Ex. Doc.,* 256, 24 Cong., 1 Sess., *passim.*

7. *House Ex. Doc.* 256, 24 Cong., 1 Sess., VI, pp. 40 *et seq.*

8. *House Ex. Doc.* 256, 24 Cong., 1 Sess., VI, pp. 15-26 ; *House Ex. Doc.* 2, 24 Cong., 2 Sess., p. 27.

9. *House Ex. Doc.* 256, 24 Cong., 1 Sess., VI, p. 32.

. . . the orders given to General Gaines were not given because the United States believed they had claims to the territory beyond Nacogdoches, nor with a view to assert, strengthen, or maintain those claims, but simply and exclusively to prevent consequences likely to grow out of the bloody contest begun in that quarter.[10]

Notwithstanding such assurances, it is not surprising, when one reads some of the communications from Gaines of which the following is typical, that Gorostiza was not entirely convinced—

Believing it to be of great importance to our country, as well as to Texas and Mexico, and indeed to the whole people of the continent of America, that our Government should be prepared to act promptly upon the anticipated application of the people of Texas for admission; and desiring, as fervently as any one of the early friends of the President can possibly desire, that this magnificent acquisition to our Union should be made within the period of his presidential term, and apprehending that unlooked for changes and embarrassing interference by foreign Powers might result from delaying our national action upon the subject to another session of Congress, I have taken leave to order to the city of Washington Captain E. A. Hitchcock . . . whose discriminating mind and perfect integrity and honor will enable him to communicate more fully than my present delicate health . . . will allow me to write, the facts and circumstances connected with this interesting subject, the opinions and wishes of the inhabitants of the eastern border of Texas, together with the late occurrences, and present state of my command.[11]

The continued reports of the passage of armed forces from the United States to Texas, and the apparent negligence of the United States in preventing these movements, together with the activities of Gaines, were noted carefully

---

10. *House Ex. Doc.* 256, 24 Cong., 1 Sess., p. 256.
11. Gaines to Cass, May 10, 1836, *House Ex. Doc.* 25 Cong., 2 Sess., XII, Doc. 351, pp. 786-787; Marshall, T. M., *A History of the Western Boundary of the Louisiana Purchase. 1819-1841*, p. 171.

by Gorostiza and drew forth numerous complaints from him during the year 1836.[12] In the latter part of 1836, he indignantly terminated his mission to the United States. Before leaving, he published a pamphlet setting forth the reasons for his action and bitterly complaining of the attitude taken by the United States in the Texas question. This was considered defamatory to the United States as well as a violation of the laws of diplomacy. A note was immediately sent to Mr. Ellis informing him of the affair and ordering him to break off diplomatic relations unless the Mexican Government disavowed the act of its minister.[13] This order did not reach Ellis until he had already demanded his passports for the reasons stated above. Thus diplomatic relations between the two countries were severed almost simultaneously in the two capitals at the close of 1836.

To the country at large war seemed imminent; but among the officials of government the matter was not considered very serious. It was determined that one more demand should be made upon Mexico for a settlement of claims.[14] The demand was sent shortly after the accession of Van Buren to the presidency.

The opposition party in Congress used the entire episode as capital for attacks on the government. Adams made his famous speech in the House, in which the entire policy of the government of the United States toward Mexico was reviewed. He declared:

> From the battle of San Jacinto, every movement of the Administration of the Union appears to have been made for the express purpose of breaking off negotiations and precipitating a war or of frightening Mexico by menaces into cession of not only Texas but of the whole course of the Rio del Norte, and five degrees of latitude across the continent to the South Sea.[15]

12. *House Ex. Doc.*, 2, 24 Cong., 2 Sess., *passim.* See Marshall, 186 *et seq.*
13. *House Ex. Doc.* 105, 24 Cong., 2 Sess., pp. 47-50.
14. *Congressional Globe*, 24 Cong., 2 Sess. IV, p. 193.
15. Adams, J. Q., *Speech on the Right of Petition, Freedom of Speech and Debate*, etc., *delivered in the House from June 16 to July 7, 1838.*

This speech gave excellent material for agitation to Mexico and the anti-slavery interest in the United States.

A careful study of the documents shows that Adams' anti-slavery proclivities, which made him read into official acts a determination to extend the slave area by fair means or foul, greatly distorted his perspective. Jackson was certainly eager to acquire Texas; but it cannot be shown that he stooped to any under-handed measures. The same can be said of Van Buren. Reeves states:

> Jackson's and Van Burean's attitude toward Texan annexation was cautious, prudent, and founded on just principles. That the tone adopted toward Mexico upon the subject of claims was severe does not thereby convict Jackson and Van Buren of duplicity or hypocrisy or shamelessness. ... Instead of using the Mexican claims as a cloak for war by which annexation might be accomplished, the reverse may be stated as the truth. The open refusal of the United States to accept the Texan offer of annexation put the United States in a position where demand for payment of its claims upon Mexico could be made without any suspicion of ulterior motive.[16]

Arbitration of Claims. On September 11, 1838, arbitration of the claims was agreed upon and all danger of war was over. Diplomatic relations were at once re-established. After some delay in preliminary arrangements, the board began its work at Washington on December 29, 1840.[17] Two commissioners had been appointed for each side and the King of Prussia through a delegate, Baron Roenne, then minister resident of Prussia at Washington, acted as umpire. In the eighteen months (August 1840-

---

16. Reeves, J. R., *American Diplomacy under Tyler and Polk*, 84-86. Kohl, *Claims as a Cause of the Mexican War*, 30-44.

17. The convention signed in 1838 was not carried into effect because of Mexico's failure to authorize the exchange of ratifications within the time prescribed. The delay was said to be due to the fact that the King of Prussia had not consented to appoint an umpire as had been provided by the terms of the convention. A second convention was concluded in April, 1839. (Moore, J. B., *International Arbitrations*, II, 1218).

February, 1842) allowed by the terms of the convention eighty-four claims had been presented and of these thirty had not been finally decided. Every evidence goes to prove the sincerity of the Mexican commissioners and their earnest efforts to adjudicate the claims according to strict justice. The amount allowed, approximately thirty per cent of the claims, was a very large proportion for such cases, and the Mexican delegates declared that failure to settle more claims was due to the tardiness with which the claimants presented their cases.[18]

The poverty of the Mexican treasury at the time rendered it impossible to pay the indemnity agreed upon. This necessitated another convention which was concluded at the city of Mexico in 1843. It was therein provided that the Mexican government should "on the thirtieth of the following April pay all interest then due on the awards, and within five years from that day, in equal installments every three months, all the principal and accruing interest."

18. An idea of the work of the commission may be gained from the following table:

	Amount
Amount of claims decided by the board without reference to the umpire	
Amount claimed	$595,462.75
Amount allowed	439,393.82
Rejected on their merits at the board	
Amount claimed	51,492.25
Decided by the board not to be within the convention	
Amount claimed	9,278.26
Claims on which the board differed which were reported to the umpire for decision, and on which allowance was made	
Amount claimed	5,844,260.44
Amount allowed by American commis.	2,334,477.44
Amount allowed by Mexican commiss.	191,012.94
Amount allowed by the umpire	1,586,745.86
Rejected by the umpire on the merits	
Amount claimed	59,967.40
Amount claimed by American commissioners	57,754.42
Decided by the umpire not to be within the cognizance of the board	
Amount claimed	1,864,939.56
Amount allowed by American commissioners	928,627.88
Cases submitted too late to be considered by the board	
Amount claimed	3,336,837.05

Total awarded by the umpire _____$1,586,745.86
Total awarded by the American commissioners on reference to the umpire 2,334,477.44
Total awarded by the Mexican commissioners on reference to the umpire 191,012.94
(Moore, op. cit., II, 1232.)

In April, 1844, the Mexican government ceased to pay installments. There was no money in the Mexican treasury, although the government had gone to the extent of demanding a forced loan with which to meet its obligations. Shortly after, a revolution caused the permanent cessation of all payments.[19] Again the diplomatic sky looked threatening; the storm was brewing in another quarter also.

The Texas Question. The question of Texan annexation was to furnish the basis of renewed difficulties with Mexico. Tyler came to the presidency determined on expansion. Was not expansion a necessity, if anything was to be accomplished in regard to the proposed opening of trade with China, and the establishment of a consul at the Sandwich Islands?[20] Within a few days after taking the oath of office, the President referred to annexation as the all important measure of his administration.[21]

In January, 1843, Mr. Thompson, the American minister to Mexico, was instructed to remonstrate against the mode of warfare which was being carried on against Texas, and to make it clear that if Texas were not either reconquered by Mexico, according to the regular mode of warfare by a sufficiently strong force, or else her independence recognized by Mexico, the United States would show her disapproval in a more forcible manner.[22]

The attitude adopted by Tyler is excellently summed up by Kohl in the statement: "Tyler's first plan for securing territory appears to have been one which very few at that time knew anything about. This was to trade the claims for Texas and California. Thompson's first dispatch to Washington, dated April 29, 1842, went aside from the main subject with which it dealt to discuss the question of acquiring territory. He declared:

19. Moore, J. B., *International Arbitrations*, II, 1216-1248. *(Ho. Mis. Doc.* 53 Cong., 2 Sess., No. 212, II, 3267). The matter was finally settled by the Treaty of Guadalupe-Hidalgo by which the United States assumed these obligations of Mexico.
20. For this interesting aspect of western extension see Lyon G. Tyler, *The Letters and Times of The Tylers II*, 262.
21. *Ibid.*, 254.
22. *Sen. Doc.* 341, 28 Cong., 1 Sess., 69-70.

I believe that this Government would cede to us Texas and the Californias, and I am thoroughly satisfied that it is all we shall ever get for the claims of our merchants on this country. As to Texas, I regard it as of little value compared with California—the richest, the most beautiful and the healthiest country in the world . . . In addition to which California is destined to be the granary of the Pacific. It is a country in which slavery is not necessary and therefore if that is made an objection, let there be another compromise. France and England both have had their eyes upon it . . . If I could mingle any selfish feelings with interests to my country so vast, I would desire no higher honor than to be an instrument in securing it.[23]

Later dispatches reveal the anxiety of Thompson to see the matter favorably adjusted.

The enmity aroused in Mexico by the evident sympathy of Americans with the Texans, together with the foolish act of Commodore Jones of the Pacific Squadron in taking possession of Monterey,[24] made impossible the acquisition of territory in exchange for claims; and Tyler did not intend to go to war for such a cause.

Agitation throughout the country continued, however, and during the last months of Tyler's administration official notice was given by the Mexican minister, Almonte, that the annexation of Texas by the United States would be considered as equivalent to a declaration of war, and in such an event he would consider his mission to the United States ended, since on receipt of the news of such an act, Mexico would immediately declare war.[25]

The stand was at once taken in Washington that the declaration of war by Mexico, if Texas were annexed, would be entirely uncalled for, since Texas had maintained her independence for eight years, and the inability of Mexico

---

23. Ms. Archives, Dept. of State, Dispatches from Agents in Mexico as cited in Kohl, *Claims as a Cause of the Mexican War*, 46.
24. For an account of the episode see *House Ex. Doc.* 166, 27 Cong., 3 Sess., *passim.*
25. *House Ex. Doc.* 2, 28 Cong., 1 Sess., pp. 39 *et seq.*

to reconquer her during all that time made it impossible for the United States to consider her longer a part of Mexico.[26]

In the closing months of his administration, Tyler strove earnestly to have the Treaty of Annexation completed and had the satisfaction of seeing this done on March 3, 1845, one day before his authority ceased, although the full ratification took place only in December, 1845, under the Polk administration. As threatened, the Mexican minister at once withdrew from Washington; and thus diplomatic relations which had so recently been restored were once more severed.[27]

Expansionist Plans of Polk. Polk, the successor of Tyler in the presidential office, showed, from the outset of his term, a great desire for expansion. He determined to attempt to re-establish amicable relations with Mexico for this purpose. Mr. Parrott was sent to determine whether or not Mexico was willing to renew diplomatic intercourse. Polk records in his diary:

> He, Parrott, is of the opinion that the government is desirous to re-establish diplomatic relations with the United States and that a minister from the United States would be received ... After much consultation, in full Cabinet, it was agreed unanimously that it was expedient to reopen diplomatic relations with Mexico, but that it was to be kept a profound secret that such a step was contemplated.[28]

The secrecy was due to fear of foreign interference. It was determined to appoint to the difficult office Mr. Slidell who seemed well qualified for the task. Before sending Slidell, assurance was procured from the Mexican Minister of Foreign affairs that Mexico would receive a Commissioner having full power to settle the Texas dispute.[29]

---

26. *Sen. Doc.* 341, 28 Cong., 1 Sess., p. 87.
27. For a detailed discussion of Annexation see McCormac, E. I., *James K. Polk, a Political Biography,* 352-72.
28. *Polk, Diary, Sept. 16, 1845.*
29. *House Ex. Doc.* 60, 30 Cong., 1 Sess., VII, pp. 13-17.

Although an important question to be settled was that of the boundary of Texas, the anxiety and hope of the Government to obtain possession of New Mexico and California are revealed in the specific instructions to Slidell upon the subject. The whole question of claims was reviewed at great length and the following conclusion reached:

The result of the whole is, that the injuries and outrages committed by the authorities of Mexico on American citizens, which, in the opinion of President Jackson, would so long ago as February, 1837, have justified a resort to war or reprisals for redress, yet remain wholly unredeemed excepting only the comparatively small amount received under the convention of April, 1839.

. . . The fact is but too well known to the world that the Mexican government is not now in a condition to satisfy these claims by the payment of money. Unless the debt should be assumed by the government of the United States, the claimants cannot receive what is justly their due. Fortunately the joint resolution of Congress, approved 1st. March, 1845, for annexing Texas to the United States, presents the means of satisfying these claims, in perfect consistency with the interests as well as the honor of both republics. It has reserved to this government the adjustment of all questions of boundary that may arise with other governments. This question of boundary may, therefore, be adjusted in such a manner between the two republics as to cast the burden of the debt due to American claimants upon their own government whilst it will do no injury to Mexico.

There follows a detailed discussion of the question of the Texas boundary, and then the interest in New Mexico asserts itself. The instructions continue:

The long and narrow valley of New Mexico, or Santa Fe, is situated on both banks of the upper Del Norte, and is bounded on both sides by mountains. It is many hundred miles remote from other settled portions of Mexico, and from its distance it is both difficult and expensive to defend the inhabitants against the tribes of fierce and warlike savages, that roam over the surrounding country. For this cause it has suffered severely from their incursions. Mexico must expend far more in defending so distant a possession, than she can possibly derive benefit from continuing to hold it.

Besides it is greatly to be desired that our boundary with Mexico should now be established in such a manner as to preclude all future difficulties and disputes between the two republics. A great portion of New Mexico being on this side of the Rio Grande, and included within the limits already claimed by Texas, it may hereafter, should it remain a Mexican province, become a subject of dispute and a source of bad feeling between those, who, I trust are destined in future to be always friends.

On the other hand, if, in adjusting the boundary, the province of New Mexico should be included within the limits of the United States, this would obviate the danger of future collisions. Mexico would part with a remote and detached province, the possession of which can never be advantageous to her; and she would be relieved from the trouble and expense of defending its inhabitants against the Indians. Besides she would thus purchase security against their attacks on her other provinces west of the Del Norte as it would at once become the duty of the United States to restrain the savage tribes within their limits, and prevent them from making hostile incursions into Mexico From these considerations, and others which will readily suggest themselves to your mind, it would seem to be equally the interest of both powers that New Mexico should belong to the United States.[30]

Slidell was instructed to offer a sufficiently large sum of money to compensate Mexico for this cession. Fear was expressed that Mexico might be contemplating the sale of California to England, and we read:

The possession of the bay and harbor of San Francisco is all important to the United States.

---

30. *Ho. Ex. Doc.* 30 Cong., 1 Sess., pp. 37-40.

The advantages to us of its acquisition are so striking that it would be a waste of time to enumerate them here. If all these should be turned against our country by the cession of California to Great Britain, our principal commercial rival, the consequences would be most disastrous.

The government of California is now but nominally dependent upon Mexico, and it is more than doubtful whether her authority will ever be reinstated. Under these circumstances, it is the desire of the President that you should use your best efforts to obtain the cession of that province from Mexico to the United States. Could you accomplish this object you would render immense service to your country and establish an enviable reputation for yourself. Money would be no object when compared with the value of the acquisition . . . Should you, after sounding the Mexican authorities on the subject, discover a prospect of success, the President would not hesitate to give, in addition to the assumption of the just claims of our citizens on Mexico, $25,000,000 for the cession.[31]

But such roseate dreams were destined to come to naught, for the United States, with her usual promptness, complied so quickly with the permission to send a minister, that Slidell reached Mexico before President Herrera had an opportunity to prepare the minds of the Mexican people for the restoration of friendly relations with the United States. The civil war which was brewing threatened the Herrera administration, and it was felt that the reception of Slidell would precipitate the dreaded disruption.[32] Events proved the instability of the President's power and justification of his fears.

The fact that, contrary to the agreement of Mexico, Slidell had been commissioned as minister plenipotentiary with power and instructions to negotiate matters other than the Texas boundary dispute and that his appointment had

---

31. *Ho. Ex. Doc.* 69, 30 Cong., 1 Sess., p. 41.
32. Brooks, N. C., *Complete History of the Mexican War,* 60.

not been confirmed by the Senate, was seized upon as an excuse for refusing to receive him.[33] The action of the United States in this matter raised a storm of protest among the Mexican patriots who saw herein the attempt of a powerful nation to take advantage of a weak neighbor and, under the guise of friendship, deprive her of her fairest provinces. The well formulated arguments did not appeal to them.

Reports from Slidell made it seem certain that he would not be received by the Mexican Government. On January 13, 1846, Polk ordered the United States' troops to advance to the Rio Grande presumably for the purpose of protecting Texas.[34] The army left Corpus Christi and reached Point Isabel on the twenty-fourth.[35] These war-like preparations could leave no doubt as to the determination of the United States to reach a solution of the difficulties that had so long existed between the two countries. On March 12, 1846, Slidell received a decided refusal from the newly formed Mexican Government, under Paredes, to receive him. Great indignation was expresesd in Mexico because of the hostile attitude assumed by the United States at the time when, presumably, it was seeking a re-establishment of diplomatic relations.[36] American writers who have studied the matter seriously have expressed divergent opinions on the Slidell mission. J. S. Reeves states:

> Parrott's mission and Slidell's instructions taken together prove two things (1) that the Mexican War was not the result of the annexation of Texas, and (2) that the reopening of diplomatic relations with Mexico was for the purpose of securing California by purchase . . . The President developed a plan by which he believed that expansion could be effected by peaceful means. Claims against Mexico under discussion as far back as Jackson's time furnished the groundwork of the

---

33. *Ho. Ex. Doc.* 60, 30 Cong., 1 Sess. VII, pp. 23-31.
34. McCormac, *op. cit.*, 375.
35. Garrison, G. P., *Westward Extension*, 222.
36. *Ho. Ex. Doc.* 60, 30 Cong., 1 Sess., VII, pp. 67 *et seq.*

plan; the joint resolution of annexing Texas gave the President something to build upon. Mexico could not pay the claims in cash; the Texan boundary was unsettled. The idea of territorial indemnity was an irresistable conclusion: let her pay in land.[37]

Failure of Diplomacy. On the reception of the news of Slidell's rejection, Polk suggested to his cabinet that a more decisive attitude be adopted toward Mexico.[38] The Oregon question then under discussion caused hesitation until Saturday, May 9, when, as Polk records in his diary, it was unanimously agreed that if any act of hostility were committed by the Mexican forces against General Taylor's forces, he should immediately recommend to Congress a declaration of war. He felt that sufficient cause had already been given, and that without waiting for further provocation, he should recommend the declaration of war on the following Tuesday. All agreed to this except Mr. Bancroft, the Secretary of the Navy, who held that war should be declared only on the commission of a definite act of hostility by the Mexican forces.[39]

Before the day was over a report of an opportune "act of hostility" was received from General Taylor giving account of the well known episode of the attack by the Mexican forces on the detachment of Taylor's troops on the eastern bank of the Rio Grande. Monday, May 11, the war message was sent to Congress, was approved, and war declared on the next day. Diplomatic efforts, of more or less sincerity, had failed. The appeal to arms was resorted to. The keynote words of Polk's message soon resounded far and wide. ". . . Mexico has shed American blood on American soil."[40]

Polk assumed much in proclaiming that the Mexican forces had entered within American territory. That he hon-

37. Reeves, J. S., *American Diplomacy under Tyler and Polk*, 275. See comment by McCormac, *op. cit.*, p. 391.
38. Polk, *Diary*, Apr. *25,1846.*
39. *Ibid., May 9, 1846.*
40. Richardson, *Messages and Papers of the Presidents, IV*, 437.

estly considered the Rio Grande as the boundary of Mexico, is doubtful.[41] Senator Benton in reviewing this affair remarks. "The march to the Rio Grande brought on the collision of arms, but so far from being the cause of the war, it was itself the effect of these causes."[42]

It would take us too far afield to enter even a brief discussion of the various causes of the Mexican war. It cannot be doubted that the question of claims is a factor to be reckoned with, but as Kohl says: "Had it not been for the ideals of expansion the claims would have been far too insignificant for notice and the Mexican War would probably have never been fought. As it was, the claims remained a constant grievance against Mexico down to the time of Polk; and he used them as a pretext, not a cause, to get indemnity in the form of territory."[43]

41. For a masterly discussion of the boundary question see, G. P. Garrison, *Texas*, pp. 262 *et seq.*

42. Benton, *Thirty Years' View II*. 639. A recent discussion of this question is given in McCormac, *op. cit.*, Ch. XVII-XVIII.

43. *Claims as a Cause of the Mexican War*, 79.

CHAPTER IV

THE MILITARY CONQUEST

Both sides entered the war with unclouded faith in its own success, and yet neither country was in the remotest state of preparation. The activities of Generals Scott and Taylor are generally considered the important events of the conflict. This is doubtless true from the standpoint of military achievement, but the success of the "Army of the West" under General Kearny was of prime strategic significance. This detachment was apparently watched with keen interest by the administration. During the earliest discussions with the Secretary of War and General Scott, Polk gave as his opinion that the first movement should be to march a competent force into the Northern Provinces and seize and hold them until peace was made. All agreed in this opinion.[1]

"The Army of the West." An order, dated June 3, communicated to Colonel, afterwards Brigadier-General, S. W. Kearny, that he was appointed to take command of the expedition destined for the conquest of Upper California. He was ordered to take possession of Santa Fe, en route, garrison it, and press on to California. One thousand mounted men had been ordered to follow him in the direction of Santa Fe, and his force was also to be increased by the incorporation of a large body of Mormons then on their way to California for the purpose of establishing homes. The number of the latter was to be limited to not more than one-third of his entire force. Kearny was ordered to establish temporary civil governments in the places which he should conquer, and, as far as possible, retain in service those who had held office under the Mexican regime and who were willing to take the oath of allegiance to the United States; to assure the people of the provinces that the design of the government was to provide a free government as soon as possible. He was warned to adopt a conciliatory

---

1. Polk, *Diary, May 14, 1846.*

attitude in every possible respect and that trade with the United States was not to be interrupted under the changed conditions.[2]

Kearny's army, as ordered to rendezvous at Fort Leavenworth, twenty-two miles above the mouth of the Kansas, comprised 1,658 men—two batteries of artillery under Major Clark, three squadrons of the First Dragoons under Major Sumner, the first regiment of Missouri cavalry under Colonel Doniphan, and two companies of infantry under Captain Agney. The various detachments came together, however, only a short distance from Bent's Fort, near the present village of Las Animas. Here they found 414 loaded wagons of the Santa Fe Trade awaiting protection.[3]

When news reached Santa Fe that the American army was encamped at Bent's Fort, a meeting of the principal citizens was called for the purpose of discussing the most effective measures to be taken. Opinions differed, some preferred to surrender without resistance; others insisted that a stand should be made against the enemy. The latter ruled. General Armijo, assisted by Pino and Baca, was entrusted with the defense. General Armijo only reluctantly approved of the plans and issued a proclamation calling upon the people of New Mexico to assist in the preservation of the Mexican State.[4]

In words of staunch loyalty which later acts contradicted, he appealed to their patriotism and loyalty, recalling the recent formation of the Republic. One paragraph is quite indicative of the whole: "The eagle that summoned you at Iguala under the national standard forming a single family out of us all, with one single will, calls on you today to gather around the supreme government . . . You then could conquer without external help, led only by your noble efforts and heroic patriotism, the independence of our

2. Sec. of War, W. L. Marcy to Gen. Kearny June 3, 1846. *House Ex. Doc. 60,* 30 Cong., 1 Sess., p. 153 ; also *House Ex. Doc. 17,* 31 Cong., 1 Sess., pp. 236-239.

3. Emory, W. H. *Notes of a Military Reconnoissance,* 14. (*Ho. Ex. Doc. 41,* 30 Cong., 1 Sess.) ; Prince, *Concise History of New Mexico,* 178.

4. Proclamation in B. M. Read Collection, D. No. 20.

nation . . . Today that sacred boon, the fruit of so many and so costly sacrifices is threatened; for if we are not able to preserve the integrity of our Territory, all this country would very soon be the prey of the greed and enterprising spirit of our neighbors on the north, and nothing would remain save a sad remembrance of our political existence."[5]

Three days after the Army of the West arrived at the Fort, Kearny dispatched Captain Cooke with twelve picked men, accompanied by James Magoffin of Kentucky, formerly American Consul in Chihuahua, and Senor Gonzales of Chihuahua, who were engaged in the caravan trade, with a flag of truce to Santa Fe, two hundred miles distant.[6]

Senator Benton has written, in his Thirty Years' View, an account of the conquest of New Mexico in which he offers an explanation of the remarkable success of Kearny. He attributes the ease of the conquest to his own wisdom in persuading James Magoffin, who was intimately acquainted with the people and conditions in New Mexico, to join himself to Kearny's army. The President and Secretary of War gladly accepted Magoffin's proffered services.[7] He accompanied Captain Cooke to Santa Fe to use his power to persuade Armijo not to resist the American force. Magoffin, it seems, obtained this promise readily enough, but had more difficulty in so persuading Colonel Archuleta, the second in command. According to Benton, Archuleta was won over to the American cause by the suggestion that he take possession for himself of the western half of New Mexico since Kearny was only going to take possession of the left bank of the Rio Grande. Pleased with this plan, which fell in so well with his ambition, Archuleta consented not to offer resistance.[8]

---

5. *Idem.* See also Ritch I, 232.

6. Cooke, P. St. George, *The Conquest of New Mexico and California,* 6; Twitchell, *The Military Occupation of New Mexico,* 376. Magoffin had been active in the Santa Fe trade at least as early as 1839. (Ritch I, 179.)

7. *Ho. Ex. Doc.* 17, 31 Cong., 1 Sess., 240-241.

8. Benton, *Thirty Years' View II,* 683. Magoffin's services were again successful in opening the way to Chihuahua for General Wool. Here he was suspected and imprisoned, returning to Washington only after peace was signed.

It is difficult to determine the actual services rendered by Magoffin and to what extent Kearny's "bloodless conquest" was made possible by him. Benton's enmity toward Kearny caused him to make as little as possible of Kearny's own work, and to exaggerate that of his assistants. In secret session of congress, Magoffin received, at Benton's plea, $30,000.[9]

"The Unbloody Conquest." The main body of the army moved forward by way of Raton Pass. Shortly after crossing the Sapello river,[10] Kearny received a message from Armijo stating that the people had risen en masse, but that he would meet Kearny on the plains between the Sapello and the Vegas.[11] Whether as friend or foe was not stated.

At Las Vegas was enacted a scene which was repeated in essentials at various points within the province of New Mexico. Kearny with his staff, riding into the public square in the early morning, was met by the alcalde and people. Ascending to the roof of one of the nearby adobe houses where all could see and hear, Kearny through the interpreter, Robidoux[12] addressed the assembled multitude, an-

---

9. The Magoffin Papers in the files of the Historical Society of New Mexico are transcripts obtained by Mr. R. E. Twitchell of the letters written by Magoffin to justify his claim to government remuneration. He does not hesitate to take to himself almost complete credit for persuading the New Mexican officials not to offer resistance. He states: "I certainly made no contract with the Government, nor did any such idea enter my head. I engaged at the request of President Polk to go to Mexico where I had been for many years, to be of service to our troops. . . . I went into Santa Fe ahead of Gen'l Kearny and smoothed the way to his bloodless conquest of New Mexico. Col. Archuletti would have fought; I quieted him. It was he who afterwards made the revolt which was put down with much bloodshed by Gen'l Price. Fight was in him, and it would have to come out at first, carrying Armijo with him if it had not been for my exertions. . . . Bloodless possession of New Mexico was what President Polk wished. It was obtained through my means. I could state exactly how I drew off Archuletti from his intention to fight." The papers in which Magoffin says he was explicit in his statement are not available. His expenditures, according to the itemized list which he sent to the War Department, amounted to $37,780.96. He states: "The above is submitted not as an account against the United States but as data to assist in forming an opinion of the amount that ought to be paid for my services, by showing what they cost me; as for the services themselves they cannot be valued in money" *(Magoffin Papers.* New Mexico Historical Society.)

10. It was here that Kearny was presented with his commission as brigadier-general.

11. Emory, *Notes of a Military Reconnoissance,* Sen. Ex. Doc. 7, 30 Cong., 1 Sess., p. 25.

12. Hughes, J. T., *Doniphan's Expedition,* 33.

nouncing that the American forces came by order of the government of Washington to take possession of New Mexico and extend over it the laws of the United States; that they came not as conquerors, but as protectors for the benefit of the people; that the authority of General Armijo had ceased and that he himself was now the governor. He assured all who submitted peacefully to the new order of things that they would be protected in their religion, their persons, and their property, but that those who were found in arms against the United States would be summarily punished. His words were given added weight by the presence of the army. He then administered the oath of allegiance and of office to the former office-holders, who accepted the inevitable with apparently no satisfaction.[13]

Leaving Las Vegas, the advance was continued with no opposition. At Tecolote and at San Miguel, scenes similar to that at Las Vegas were enacted. On the way thither various persons had been met who reported that Armijo was assembling his forces, and that a vigorous resistance might be expected at a place fifteen miles from Santa Fé called the Cañon, which was being fortified.[14] At San Miguel a rumor reached Kearny that the two thousand Mexicans assembled in the cañon to oppose his advance, had quarreled among themselves and that Armijo had fled with his forces to the south. The reporters said that Armijo, realizing the hopelessness of the situation, had been opposed to resistance from the beginning.[15]

---

13. Emory, *op. cit.*, 27 *et seq.*
14. *Ibid.*, 25.
15. Magoffin writes: "Gen. Armijo on the 15th ordered his troops, say 3,000 in number to be placed between two mountains with four pieces of artillery on the road by which our army had to pass. . . . Armijo . . . called his officers together and wished to know if they were prepared to defend the territory. They answered they were not, that they were convinced by the proclamation they had from Gen. Kearny that the U. S. had no intention to wage war with New Mexico, on the contrary promised them all protection in their property, person and religion. Armijo apparently appeared very much exasperated, gave orders to the troops to be dispersed and in 48 hours they were all at their homes, he himself leaving for the state of Chihuahua with say 100 dragoons. . . ." (Magoffin to Sec. of War, W. L. Marcy. Transcript in files of Historical Society of New Mexico.)

When at a short distance from Pecos, a letter was brought from Juan Bautista Vigil y Alarid,[16] the lieutenant-governor, informing Kearny of Armijo's flight and of Vigil's readiness to receive him in Santa Fé and extend to him the hospitalities of the city. The march was continued and the entire army arrived at Santa Fé at six o'clock on August 18. Vigil and some twenty or thirty of the people received Kearny and his staff at the palace. At sunset, the military salute greeted the American flag which had been hoisted over the building.[17]

Kearny had fulfilled the first part of his instructions. New Mexico, which repeated negotiation had failed to obtain, now became a part of the United States. Not a shot had been fired. The only lives lost were those of the men who had succumbed to the difficulties and privations of the long rapid march.

On the following morning Kearny addressed the people of Santa Fe in substantially the same words that he had used in his first proclamation on Mexican soil. Vigil answered and in the name of the entire people swore obedience and respect to the laws and authority of the United States, since "no one in this world can successfully resist the power of him who is stronger."[18]

On August 24, Kearny reported to Brigadier-General Jones, Adjutant General U. S. A., Washington, that the official proclamation had been issued and that the people

---

16. This Vigil was a cousin of the better known Donaciano Vigil of whom Twitchell says: "Captain Vigil . . . concluded that there might be relief for his people in the coming of the army of the United States. He naturally loved liberty for liberty's sake. He realized that the reforms under the Republic of Mexico so often promised would never be realized. His familiar intercourse during the generation previous with the Santa Fe trader, with 'Americans' fresh from the 'States' doubtless contributed to the determination of his course. . . . There is small doubt that the occupation of the Capital by General Kearny without the loss of life in bloody conflict was largely due to the sagacious foresight and patriotic action of Captain Vigil." (*The Military Occupation of New Mexico*, 216) Donaciano Vigil was appointed Secretary of New Mexico by Kearny (R. I., 244).

17. Emory, *Notes of a Military Reconnoissance*, p. 31 *et seq.*

18. *Vigil Papers*. Ms. New Mexico Historical Society, Santa Fe. Also R. I., 242.

of the province were quiet and could easily be kept so.[19]

The days immediately following were employed in receiving delegations from the Pueblo Indians and from Taos, in providing for the well being of the soldiers, and in arranging for the construction of Fort Marcy, named after the Secretary of War. This fort was situated on a hill which commanded the entire town. It was built by the volunteers, who considered it a real hardship to be put to a work of such a character when they had entered the army to fight and so far had no chance to show their military powers. It was felt, however, that this fort which when completed could accommodate one thousand soldiers and was armed with fourteen cannon, was extremely necessary, since Kearny intended, according to his instructions, to take the greater part of the army to California.[20]

Rumors now reached Santa Fe that Armijo and Colonel Ugarte were assembling forces in the south and marching toward the capital. Kearny, at the head of seven hundred men, marched down the Rio Grande to Tomé, one hundred miles distance, but met with no hostile demonstrations.[21]

Kearny's Code. On his return to Santa Fe Kearny, in consonance with his instructions, appointed the civil officers, with Charles Bent as governor. Many of those chosen had held office under Mexican rule, but were doubtless of partial American extraction as revealed by their names.[22] He also

---

19. *Ho. Ex. Doc.* 19, 29 Cong., 2 Sess.
20. Prince, L. B., *History of New Mexico*, 299.
21. Cutts, *The Conquest of California and New Mexico*, 64.
22. "In 1853 Mr. Phelps, a member of Congress speaking of the officials of the government set up by Kearny in place of the one he had over-thrown, said that they were Americans residing in New Mexico. While this was true in part, it is likely to create a wrong impression. They were not mere adventurers. Some of them had resided there many years, ten or fifteen, and had become bound to the country by marital and other ties. This was true of the governor, Charles Bent, a native of Virginia, who had been in New Mexico since 1832 . . . Francis P. Blair, Jr., district attorney, was a member of the Missouri Blair family and was afterwards prominent in public life at Washington. Two members of the supreme court, Joab Houghton and Charles Beaubien, were Americans, but the latter had been a resident of Taos, New Mexico, since 1827, had married a native, and was widely known and respected . . . Nearly all the others . . . were natives, some of them members of prominent families." (Thomas, D. Y., *A History of Military Government in Newly Acquired Territory of the United States*, 115-116.)

announced a plan of civil government. In his report on the
laws drawn up, Kearny foregoes any credit for himself and
acknowledges that he was entirely indebted for them to
Colonel A. W. Doniphan of the Missouri mounted volunteers, who was assisted by W. P. Hall of his regiment. The
laws were taken from several sources: from the laws of
Mexico, either retained in their original form or modified
to bring them into agreement with the laws of the United
States; from the laws of Texas and of Texas-Coahuila;
from the statutes of Missouri, and the Livingston Code.
The organic law was taken from the organic law of Missouri
territory.[23] This code was later the subject of violent debate
in the House and was used as a weapon with which to
attack the administration on the entire subject of the war.[24]
Kearny doubtless had no thought of over-stepping his instructions.

Having established order in Santa Fe, General Kearny
set out, on the twenty-fifth, for California. Colonel Doniphan was left in command of all the forces in New Mexico
with orders to march against Chihuahua on the arrival of
Colonel Price,[25] who was daily expected with his detachment
which consisted of 1,200 mounted volunteers from Missouri
and a Mormon battalion of 500 infantry which had been
organized at Council Bluffs. When, after a few days, this
new addition was made to the force already in Santa Fe,
the town was transformed into a military camp. In all,
there were now 3,500 men stationed there.[26] Doniphan
received orders from Kearny, then at La Joya, to postpone
his previously ordered march to Chihuahua and as quickly
as possible march against the Navajo Indians who were
making depredations on territory now belonging by right of
conquest to the United States. Doniphan complied at once
and Colonel Price was left in command at Santa Fe.

---

23. *Ho. Ex. Doc.* 60, 30 Cong., 1 Sess., p. 176.
24. For debate see *Congressional Globe*, 29 Cong., 2 Sess., Dec. 7, 1846, pp. 33
et seq., Thomas, 106-117.
25. Hughes, J. T., *Doniphan's Expedition*, 51.
26. Twitchell, R. E., *Military Occupation of New Mexico*, 95.

The Revolt of 1846. When Colonel Price took over the command, he immediately stationed the divisions of his forces in various parts of New Mexico as well for the good of the men themselves, as for the preservation of order and submission among the New Mexicans and the Pueblo Indians.[27]

Although Kearny was confident that the people of New Mexico were satisfied with the new condition of things, murmurs of revolt were heard almost immediately after his departure for California and of Doniphan to the south.

The more influential of the Mexicans who had formerly held positions of honor and who now found themselves the objects of the scorn of the invaders naturally chafed under the new conditions. To them, particularly, it seemed but patriotism to drive out those who were holding the country by force.[28]

No definite benefit had, as yet, resulted from the American occupation, and the overbearing, abusive, and quarrelsome actions of the volunteers made them and the country they represented obnoxious in the extreme.[29] Ruxton, an English traveler, reports, "I found over all New Mexico that the most bitter feeling and most determined hostility existed against the Americans who, certainly in Santa Fe and elsewhere, have not been very anxious to conciliate the people, but by their bullying and overbearing demeanor toward them, have in a great measure been the cause of this hatred."[30]

Among the most prominent instigators of rebellion was Diego Archuleta. It is possible, as Senator Benton suggests, that his hostility could be traced to his disappointment in not being allowed to control the western half of New Mex-

---

27. Hughes, J. T., *Doniphan's Expedition*, 138.
28. Prince, L. B., *Historical Sketches of New Mexico*, 313.
29. Bancroft, *Arizona and New Mexico*, 431.
30. Ruxton, G. F., *Wild Life in the Rocky Mountains*, 75. For a detailed account of the disorderly behavior of the soldiers in New Mexico see J. H. Smith, *The War with Mexico*, II, pp. 216-217.

ico according to the arrangements entered into with Magoffin.[31]

Early in December the leading citizens of Santa Fe, following the lead of Thomas Ortiz and Archuleta, began definitely to plan the overthrow of the government which had been newly set up. As far as can be ascertained from the meagre accounts which have been preserved, a general massacre of the Americans and their Mexican supporters was planned. The leaders dispersed to various parts of New Mexico in order to stir up a rebellion simultaneously in all the important outlying districts and thus insure success. The night of Christmas eve was finally determined upon as the most favorable time for the assault. Plans were well laid and all seemed to promise success, but the mulatto wife of one of the conspirators revealed the plot to Donaciano Vigil who at once made it known to Colonel Price, and the incipient rebellion was at once suppressed. Many persons suspected of complicity were arrested, but the ring-leaders escaped, notwithstanding the efforts of Colonel Price to prevent this.[32]

The Taos Rebellion. While tranquility seemed to be restored, the agitators were not to be so easily discouraged. Another more formidable uprising was being secretly fomented throughout the entire province. As planned, it broke out on the nineteenth of January. Charles Bent, the governor, was murdered at his home at Taos whither he had gone from Santa Fe with a small escort, refusing to believe that his life was in any danger. Massacres of Americans took place on the same day at the Arroyo Hondo, Mora, and on the Colorado.

31. See above p. 76. With the unsatisfactory records which we possess in regard to Magoffin, this can be only conjecture.

32. This account of the rebellion, as well as the following narrative of the later revolt is based on the official report of Colonel Price to the Adjutant General of the Army February 15, 1846 as given in *Niles' Register*, 72, pp. 121-2; and J. T. Hughes, *Doniphan's Expedition* 139 *et seq.* The same may be found in various secondary works such as those of Bancroft, Prince, Read, etc. Local tradition holds that Mme. Tules the noted gambler who went to Santa Fe from Taos was the one who gave the information regarding the uprising to Colonel Price.

The wide extent of the rebellion leads one to doubt the reported willingness with which the New Mexicans had hailed the change in their government. One is led to believe that while the bonds which united New Mexico to the central government were very weak, there was not unqualified approval of the annexation of the province to the United States. Because of its distance from Mexico, which prevented any efficient protection being extended to this outlying province, a strong spirit of real independence and self-reliance had developed among the inhabitants. One evidence of this is found in the successful opposition to the repeatedly attempted imposition of the "estanquillas" or the monopoly by the general government of the sale of tobacco. Had the American government shown its ability to bestow on New Mexico what the Mexican government never could—stability of government, safety of property and personal rights together with protection from the hostile Indians, there can be no doubt that the change of authority would have been gladly received.[33] Such assurance, as we have seen, had not yet been given. The revolt and discontent also bear evidence against Mr. Dickinson of New York who, speaking in the Senate in 1848 on the justice of the Mexican War and of our acquisition of all of Mexico said ... "But whatever may be our policy touching Mexican conquests we cannot, if we would, restore New Mexico and California to that government, for the reason that they will not be restored. . . . As well return to Great Britain what was once her colonial possessions; give back Louisiana to France, Florida to Spain; Texas to Mexico."[34]

Colonel Price was at once apprised of the revolt. Through intercepted letters of the rebels, he learned that an appeal for aid was being made by the insurgents to the people of the south; that their army was marching toward Santa Fe; that their numbers were being constantly aug-

---

33. Wislizenus, A., *Memoir of a Tour to Northern Mexico.* (*Sen. Mis. Doc.* 26. 30 Cong., 1 Sess.)

34. *Congressional Globe*, 30 Cong., 1 Sess., p. 158.

mented by inhabitants of the settlements through which they passed.[35]

An immediate suppression of the uprising was determined upon. Although the inclemency of the weather and a recent heavy snow rendered military movements difficult, the American troops succeeded, after encounters at La Cañada and El Embudo, in forcing the insurgents to retreat toward Taos.[36] The bravery of the volunteers won from Colonel Price the highest praise.

At the Pueblo of Taos the Mexican and Indian forces were found firmly intrenched behind the adobe walls which seemed impervious to artillery fire. After an assault lasting over two hours, the American soldiers were withdrawn for the night. On the next day the stubborn resistance was finally overcome, and at nightfall the soldiers entered the town which formally surrendered on the following morning.[37]

Other rebellions were being crushed at the same time at smaller centres, particularly the village of Mora. An uprising at Las Vegas was prevented by the loyalty of the alcalde and his advisers. By the repeated successes of the American arms, law and order were at length reestablished. The ringleaders of the uprising, fifteen in all, were executed.[38]

Others who were accused of complicity in the plot to overthrow the American power were tried in the civil court and convicted of treason. Antonio Maria Trujillo, now an old man, was sentenced to death. This sentence was later reviewed, and Trujillo pardoned.[39] The defendants held that treason could not be imputed to Mexican citizens until a definite treaty of peace was signed between Mexico and the United States. The report of the trial of Trujillo caused

25. Copy of Official Report of Colonel Price in *Niles Register*, 72, p. 121; Donaciano Vigil to Sec. of State, J. Buchanan, *Ho. Ex. Doc.* 70, 30 Cong., 1, Sess., pp. 19-20.

36. Hughes, *Doniphan's Expedition*, 140.

37. Price, *op. cit.* 122; Garrard, L. H., *Wah-to-Yah and the Taos Trail*, 212-215.

38. Hughes, *op. cit.*, 141; Prince, L. B., *Historical Sketches of New Mexico*, 325.

39. Bancroft, H. H., *Arizona and New Mexico*, 436.

Congress to pass a resolution calling upon the President to give information as to whether anyone had been tried and condemned for treason against the United States in the newly conquered regions and if so, under what authority this tribunal had been established.[40]

The request of District Attorney, Frank P. Blair, appointed by General Kearny, for instructions as to what course to follow in view of the charge of lack of jurisdiction, brought forth the following significant reply from the Secretary of War, Marcy:

> The territory conquered by our arms does not become, by the mere act of conquest, a permanent part of the United States, and the inhabitants of such territory are not to the full extent of the term, citizens of the United States. It is beyond dispute that, on the establishment of a temporary civil government in a conquered country, the inhabitants owe obedience to it, and are bound by the laws which may be adopted. They may be tried and punished for offences. Those in New Mexico, who in the late insurrection were guilty of murder, or instigated others to that crime were liable to be punished for these acts, either by the civil or military authority; but it is not the proper use of the technical term to say that their offence was treason committed against the United States; for to the government of the United States, as the government under our constitution it would not be correct to say that they owed allegiance. It appears by the letter of Mr. Blair that those engaged in the insurrection have been proceeded against as traitors to the United States. In this respect I think there was an error so far as relates to the designation of the offence. Their offence was against the temporary civil government of New Mexico and the laws provided for it, which that government had the right and indeed was bound to see enforced. . . . You will I trust excuse an allusion to another subject not officially before me; I mean the state of discipline among our

---

40. Twitchell, R. E., *The Military Occupation of New Mexico*, 143-4.

troops at Santa Fe. Though I am far from giving
credence to the newspaper accounts in relation to
it, they ought not to pass entirely unnoticed and
may be permitted to prompt a caution on that
point.
As commanding officer you cannot err in enforcing the most rigid rules of discipline.[41]

The uprising had shown the need of increased vigilance
which was maintained during the remainder of the year.[42]
The slightest indication of rebellion was carefully noted
and suppressed. After a few weak attempts at insurrec-
tion, peace was once more assured but with increased dissatisfaction and distrust on both sides.[43]

The Treaty of Guadalupe-Hidalgo. While these problems were being worked out in New Mexico the unqualified
success of the American arms in the various quarters in
which the war was being carried on, culminating in the
occupation of Mexico City by General Scott, finally forced
the Mexican government to sue for peace. The treaty of
Guadalupe-Hidalgo drawn up on February 2, 1848, and
formally ratified at Queretaro on May 30, closed the war of
which both sides, particularly the United States, had
become weary.[44]

Notwithstanding the popular opposition to a prolonga-
tion of the war, the treaty as presented by our discredited
minister, Trist, was subjected to lengthy criticism and hot
debate in the Senate. Some were opposed to any extension
of territory "and the incorporation of the vast population
which seemed incapable of incorporation;" others, whose
expansion ideas were even more progressive than Polk's,
would stop at nothing short of the absorption of all of
Mexico in simple compensation for the claims against
Mexico; while others based their opposition on Trist's lack
of authority to negotiate a peace. Public opinion at length

41. *Ho. Ex. Doc.* 70, 30 Cong., 1 Sess., pp. 33-4.
42. Hughes, *op. cit.*, 142.
43. See Bancroft, *Arizona and New Mexico*, 438.
44. For a good discussion of the various aspects of the treaty see Klein, J., *The Making of the Treaty of Guadalupe-Hidalgo, passim.*

triumphed. By a close vote, thirty-eight to fourteen—a change of four votes would have reversed the decision—the treaty was ratified by the Senate.

The opposition to what seemed to Mexico the exorbitant demands of the victor and a total repudiation of the national honor was overcome only by the realization that in the midst of the intestine strife which was then going on, more favorable terms could not be hoped for if the war were continued.[45]

By the terms of the Treaty, the boundaries of the United States were extended to embrace all the land previously held by Mexico within the present limits of the United States, with the exception of the small district known as the Gadsden Purchase territory which was acquired later. Provision was made for the careful marking of the boundary between the two countries; the United States made herself responsible for the preservation of peace and order among the border Indian tribes; assumed the debts of Mexico to American citizens, and agreed to pay to Mexico fifteen million dollars for the ceded territory. Thus New Mexico and California became an integral part of the United States.[46] Kearny's work had not been in vain; Polk's aim was accomplished; the Pacific was our western limit.

---

45. Klein, *op. cit.*, 17-19; *Sen. Ex. Doc.* 52, 30 Cong., 1 Sess.; *Ho. Ex. Doc.* 69, 30 Cong., 1 Sess., p. 69.

46 *Ho. Ex. Doc.* 69, 30 Cong., 1 Sess., pp. 8-33.

CHAPTER V

THE INDIAN PROBLEM

The acquisition of the new territory brought to the United States an important and difficult duty. Within the confines of the region were numerous Indian tribes for whose future the federal government was now responsible. It was apparent from the outset that the plan of action adopted in New Mexico must have a two-fold aspect, for here were found two decidedly distinct types of aborigines; the wild roving tribes whose names spread terror far and wide, and the more or less civilized Pueblo Indians.

The Indians of New Mexico. Various estimates have been given of the number of Indians in New Mexico. The discrepancies in these accounts prove that they were based largely on conjecture; but at least they give some indication of the magnitude of the task with which the administrators of government were obliged to cope.

The first report after the American occupation was that given by Charles Bent, appointed Governor and ex-officio Superintendent of Indian Affairs by Kearny. It is more than probable that this approached as nearly to a correct estimate as most of the later records, since Bent, as a resident and trader in New Mexico for many years, had opportunities to make himself familiar with the true state of affairs.

He places first in his report the Apaches or Jicarillas[1] whom he describes as a band, 500 in number, of about one hundred lodges, having no permanent residence but roaming through the northern settlements of New Mexico; an indolent cowardly people living principally by theft committed on the New Mexicans since there was little game in the country and their fear of the other Indians prevented them from venturing upon the plains for the buffalo. Their

---

1. "Jicarilla (Mex. Span. 'little basket')—An Athapascan tribe first so called by the Spaniards because of their expertness in making vessels of basketry" (Hodge, F. W., *Handbook of American Indians* I, 631).

only manufacture was a species of pottery capable of resistance to fire. This they exchanged in very small quantities with the Mexicans for the necessaries of life.[2]

The Apaches proper, according to Bent, ranged through the southern portion of New Mexico through the country of the Rio del Norte and its tributaries and westward about the headwaters of the river Gila. This warlike people of about nine hundred lodges and from five thousand to six thousand persons lived almost entirely by plundering the Mexican settlements, having no knowledge of agriculture or manufactures of any kind. The maguey plant which grew without cultivation in their locality furnished a small supply of food. The amount of stock which they had successfully carried off from the Mexican settlements was incredibly large. An effort had been made by the State of Chihuahua to restrain these marauders by paying them a bounty of so much a day per head, but this had not been a success.[3]

Next in importance were the Navajoes,[4] variously estimated at seven thousand to fourteen thousand in number in from one thousand to two thousand families; "an industrious, intelligent and warlike tribe of Indians who cultivate the soil and raise sufficient grain for their own consumption and a variety of fruits." But their chief wealth consisted of flocks and herds. "It is estimated that the tribe possesses

---

2. *Report of Charles Bent in Ho. Ex. Doc. 17, 31 Cong.,* 1 *Sess.,* pp. 191-194. This report is the source for this description of the Indians of New Mexico, unless otherwise stated.

3. "While Mr. Bailey, a special agent to this tribe, agrees with the testimony of nearly all the people who had any knowledge of them, in pronouncing them the most bloodthirsty, cruel, and treacherous of all the tribes of this section . . . yet he differs from the testimony of Gov. Bent and Schoolcraft and asserts that they were not entirely nomadic, but possessed generally permanent villages in the mountain valleys north of the Gila where they cultivate the soil to a limited extent and where their women and children are beyond the reach of attacking parties" (Marsh, R. E., *The Federal Indian Policy in New Mexico 1845-60,* 11).

4. "Fray Alonso Benavides in his Memorial of 1630 gives the earliest translation of the tribal name in the form Navajo, 'sementras grandes'—'great seed sowings' or 'great fields.' The Navajo themselves do not use this name except when trying to speak English. All do not know it . . . They call themselves Dine which means simply 'people.' This word as a tribal name is used by nearly every people of the Athabascan stock." (Hodge II, 41.)

30,000 head of horned cattle, 500,000 sheep and 10,000 head of horses, mules and asses, it not being a rare instance for one individual to possess 5,000 to 10,000 sheep and 400 to 500 head of other stock, and their horses are said to be greatly superior to those raised by the Mexicans." Most of their stock had been acquired by depredations on the territory of New Mexico. The Navajo blanket, today so well known, was at that time their chief manufacture. They had no permanent villages or places of residence but wandered over a stretch of territory one hundred and fifty miles in width between the San Juan River on the north and the Gila on the south. The almost inaccessible table lands on which they dwelt, where water was scarce and found with difficulty, afforded them excellent protection against their enemies whom they successfully plundered for captives in men, women and children, to be employed as slaves. At the time of the American occupation many were so held.[5]

The form of government of the Navajoes made it difficult to deal with them for there was no central authority. Power in the tribe was usually proportional to wealth and he who could claim possession of a few head of cattle or horses demanded a voice in the government. He who did not win the approval of the vast majority of the poorer members of the tribe was apt to find himself divested of all authority. This condition made it almost impossible to locate responsibility for crime and properly punish offenders.[6]

North of the Navajoes and west of the northern settlements of New Mexico were the Yutahs [7] who, according to Bent, numbered eight hundred lodges and between four and five thousand individuals. The mountainous country in which they dwelt abounded in wild game, deer, elk, and bear, which served them for food and clothing. A hardy, warlike people, they subsisted by the chase and carried on a

5. Bent, *op. cit.*
6. *Sen. Ex. Doc.* 35 Cong., 1 Sess., Vol. II, 562.
7. Ute (Hodge II, 874).

predatory war in which they took many New Mexicans captive and drove off large amounts of stock.

These Indians were the most skillful of all the tribes in New Mexico in the use of firearms. At times some of the band would work peacefully for the New Mexicans during the threshing season but their good will could never be relied upon.[8]

Among the other wild tribes described by Bent were the Cheyennes [9] of three hundred lodges and fifteen hundred souls, and the Arapahoes, two thousand in number in four hundred lodges, who ranged through the country of the Arkansas and its tributaries on the northern part of New Mexico. They were on friendly terms with the New Mexicans with whom they carried on a trade in buffalo robes.

East of the mountains of New Mexico were the twelve thousand Comanches who lived entirely by the chase. These, too, were at peace with the New Mexicans; but caused terror in Chihuahua, Durango, and Coahuila, which they successfully invaded for captives and for herds of horses, mules and asses.

Besides these were the Cayugas whom Bent numbers as two thousand, similar in customs and habits to the Comanches but considered a braver people.

But the most interesting of all the Indians described by Bent were the Moquis,[10] one of the Pueblo group. These neighbors of the Navajoes, numbering three hundred and fifty families or two thousand four hundred and fifty individuals, lived in permanent villages, cultivating grain and fruit, raising all varieties of stock, and engaging in the same manufacturing as the Navajoes. They are described as an intelligent, industrious people. Formerly a very numerous tribe possessing large flocks and herds, at the time of the coming of the Americans, they had been

8. *Sen. Ex. Doc.* 84, 33 Cong., 2 Sess., Vol. I, 377.
9. A large part of this tribe had made permanent headquarters on the Arkansas immediately after the building of Bent's Fort, in 1832. (Hodge I, 252.)
10. Hopi (Hodge I, 560).

reduced in numbers and possessions by their warlike neighbor enemies, the Navajoes.

Deducting from the entire number given in this account five thousand as the probable number of Apaches and Comanches within the boundaries of Texas, Bent computed that there were about thirty one thousand nine hundred Indians in New Mexico.[11]

The Pueblo Indians were, without a doubt, the most important, although their pacific conduct caused them to be often overlooked by Washington while efforts were being made to restrain the marauding tribes. There were twenty pueblos or villages in New Mexico. In 1849, the Indian Agent, Calhoun, sent to Col. W. Medill, Commissioner of Indian Affairs, statistics regarding the pueblos, based on the census ordered by the Legislature of New Mexico in 1847. He computed that there were in all 6,524.[12] Although in all plans and regulations the Pueblo Indians were treated as a unit, they were, in reality, spread over an area of two hundred miles from east to west. Their languages were quite distinct and few pueblos understood that of others.[13]

In order to acquaint the government with the early history of the Pueblos, the Indian Agent, John Greiner, in 1852 presented to Calhoun, then Governor, important data concerning Spanish and Mexican laws in their regard.

The first edict on this subject was that issued by Emperor Charles V, in 1551, and later adopted by Philip II. This decree recites that the principal cause for lively interest in the natives of the New World was the desire to establish Christianity. . . It was therefore resolved "that the Indians should be brought to settle (reduced to pueblos) and that they should not live divided and separated by mountains and hills, depriving themselves of all benefit spiritual and temporal."

---

11. *Ho. Ex. Doc.* 76, 30 Cong., 1 Sess., p. 11.
12. Calhoun, Oct. 4, 1849, *op. cit.,* 39.
13. *Ibid.,* 497, 40.

In choosing a site for such a settlement, Philip II ordered that care should be taken to select a healthy place with abundance of tillable soil, "pasturage for the growth of flocks, mountains and trees for wood, materials for houses and other buildings, and water abundant and suitable for drinking and irrigation . . ."

It was also stipulated that definite assignment of land should be made to each settlement that "the sites on which pueblos and settlements were to be formed should have water privileges, lands and mountains, entrances and exits, farming lands, and a common of a league in extent, where the Indians might keep their herds without mixing with those of the Spaniards." In 1541, Charles V ordered that the pastures, mountains and waters should be common throughout the Indies.

In order to prevent the infliction of injury on the flocks or herds of the "reduced" Indians, a law of Philip III in 1618 provided that the grazing lands of large stock should not be within a league and a half of the old settlements and those of small stock less than half a league. In the new settlements the limits were to be twice as great.

To prevent advantage being taken of the ignorance and trustfulness of the Indians by those who would endeavor to obtain from them the property which had been given to them, a law was passed in Mexico in 1781 whereby it was commanded "That in no case, nor under any pretext may sales, loans, pawns, rents, nor any other kind of alienation of Indian lands be executed."[14]

How faithfully these laws were carried out most probably will never be ascertained. At least in New Mexico the Indians who were located in pueblos had made much more progress in the arts of civilization than those who were not, and it seems that their land rights were quite well respected even during the weak Mexican administration.

Beginning of Relations between the United States and the Indians of the Southwest. The conquest of Santa Fe

---

14. *Ibid.*, 497-507.

had scarcely been effected when delegations of many of
the tribes presented themselves to Kearny to show their
willingness to acknowledge the authority of the United
States. Among the first to do so were the Apaches who
glibly promised their allegiance if influence would be exerted in their behalf on their enemies, the Comanches, the
Utes, the Navajoes and the Arapahoes.[15]

On his march to California, Kearny received word that
the Navajoes were ravaging the western portion of New
Mexico. According to the promises he had made to the
citizens, he was obliged to protect the attacked. Colonel
Doniphan was therefore ordered against them. With Major
Gilpin and Lieutenant-Colonel Jackson he succeeded in
making a treaty with these "mountain lords and scourges
of New Mexico" who found it difficult to understand why
peace with the Americans should imply peace with the New
Mexicans so lately the enemy of both.[16]

Subsequent events proved that in so far as this and
other treaties of similar nature [17] were concerned, the long
wearisome march to the heart of the Indian country was
utterly useless; but it gave some definite ideas of the wealth
of the western tribes in flocks and herds, and some knowledge of the territory inhabited or roamed over by them. It
also proved to the Indians that their mountain fastnesses
were not as inaccessible to the Americans as they had
thought. This had a salutary effect for at least a very brief
space of time.

Article XI of the Treaty of Guadalupe Hidalgo. One of
the most important provisions of the treaty of Guadalupe
Hidalgo was that contained in Article XI which reads:

> Considering that a great part of the terri-
> tories which, by the present treaty, are to be com-
> prehended for the future within the limits of the
> United States is now occupied by savage tribes
> who will hereafter be under the exclusive control

15. Hughes, J. T., *Doniphan's Expedition,* 51.
16. *Ibid.,* 51-72.
17. *Ho. Ex. Doc. 5,* 31 Cong., 1 Sess., 113-115.

of the government of the United States, and whose incursions within the territory of Mexico would be prejudicial in the extreme, it is solemnly agreed that all such incursions shall be forcibly restrained by the government of the United States whensoever this may be necessary; and that they shall be punished by the same government, and satisfaction for the same shall be exacted all in the same way, and with equal diligence and energy, as if the same incursions were meditated or committed within its own territory, against its own citizens.

It shall not be lawful, under any pretext whatever, for any inhabitant of the United States to purchase or acquire any Mexican, or any foreigner residing in Mexico, who may have been captured by Indians inhabiting the territory of either of the two republics, nor to purchase or acquire horses, mules, cattle or property of any kind stolen within Mexican territory by such Indians.

And in the event of any person or persons captured within Mexican territory by Indians being carried into the territory of the United States, the government of the latter engages and binds itself, in the most solemn manner, so soon as it shall know of such captives being within its territory and shall be able to do through the faithful exercise of its influence and power to rescue them and return them to their country or deliver them to the agent or representative of the Mexican government. The Mexican authorities will, as far as practicable, give to the government of the United States notice of such captives; and its agent shall pay the expense incurred in the maintenance and transmission of the rescued captives, who, in the meantime shall be treated with the utmost hospitality by the American authorities at the place where they may be. But if the government of the United States before receiving such notice from Mexico should obtain intelligence, through any other channel, of the existence of Mexican captives within its territory it will proceed forthwith to effect their release and delivery to the Mexican agent as above stipulated.

For the purpose of giving to these stipulations the fullest possible efficiency thereby affording the security and redress demanded by their true spirit and intent, the government of the United States will now and hereafter pass, without unnecessary delay, and always vigilantly enforce, such laws as the nature of the subject may require. And finally the sacredness of this obligation shall never be lost sight of by the said government when providing for the removal of the Indians from any portion of the said territories, or for its being settled by the citizens of the United States; but on the contrary special care shall be taken not to place its Indian occupants under the necessity of seeking new homes by committing those invasions which the United States have solemnly obliged them to restrain.[18]

After prolonged debate in the Senate, this article was agreed to in its original form except the section which prohibited the furnishing of arms or ammunition to any Indian by an inhabitant of the United States. Since the Indians lived by the chase, it was argued that to deprive them of firearms would force them to resort to plunder in order to obtain sustenance.[19]

The United States thus took upon herself the three-fold task of keeping the several Indian tribes at peace with one another, protecting her own citizens and the adjacent Mexican settlements from their incursions. The physiography of the country and its extremes of climate; Mexican sympathizers residing along the border and within the limits of the United States; unscrupulous traders and "land grabbers" who had nothing but their own selfish interests as actuating principles; conflicts between state and federal, and more especially between civil and military authority; and lack of any agreement between the United States and Mexico for reciprocal crossing the border in pursuit of the ravaging bands, all these factors contributed to render well

---

18. *Ho. Ex. Doc.* 69, 30 Cong., 1 Sess., pp. 18-20.
19. *Cong., Globe,* 30 Cong., 2 Sess., p. 495.

nigh impossible an overwhelming task even under the most favorable circumstances.[20]

It is so frequently asserted that Mexico showed herself a very weak, if not stupid administrator in her inability to protect her distant settlements from the ravages of the Indians that it is rather surprising to find that little glory can justly be claimed by the United States because of its greater successes.

Events proved that the assurance of Polk, "If New Mexico were held by the United States we could prevent these tribes from committing such outrages and compel them to release the captives and restore them to their families and friends,"[21] and the confidence of Buchanan that his government had the will and the power to restrain the wild tribes,[22] were more a hope than a fact.

Conditions in New Mexico After the Conquest. Although politics colored so many of the reports of this period to such an extent that it is difficult to distinguish the true from the false, there is more reason to believe than to doubt that the conditions were worse rather than better after the conquest. The St. Louis Republican declared on November 6, 1847, that Indian depredations in New Mexico had been more destructive to life and property during the preceding year than at any other period for twenty years. This was attributed to the lack of military resistance and the fact that American traders were allowed to continue to barter their wares with the Indians who were constantly outraging the people of New Mexico.[23]

On October 4, 1848, the Superintendent of Indian Affairs had reported that fewer robberies had been committed on the travelers on the Santa Fé trail during that year than the two previous ones.[24] On February 3, 1849,

20. Rippy, J. F., *The Relations of the United States and Mexico, 1848-1860,* 112-113; Calhoun, *Correspondence, passim.*
21. *Sen. Ex. Doc. 1,* 30 Cong., 1 Sess., p. 1.
22. *Cong. Globe,* 30 Cong., 2 Sess., p. 495.
23. *Niles Register,* Nov. 6, 1847, Vol. 73, 155.
24. *Ho. Ex. Doc. I.,* 30 Cong., 2 Sess., p. 440.

Colonel Washington communicated to the War Department that there were indications that the wild tribes in the out-lying regions "were becoming convinced that they must restrain themselves within prescribed limits and cultivate the earth for an honest livelihood or be destroyed."[25]

But the Indian Agent Fitzpatrick, through whose dis-trict the trail ran, gave an explanation, which later events bore out, of the seeming submission. He would see no cause for the cessation of hostilities except that the Indians had secured so much booty in 1846 and 1847 that they were then luxuriating in the spoils. He warned against the conclusion that any real solution of the problem had been reached. Together with all that were familiar with the true condi-tions, he asserted that only by an exhibition of real power could the United States impress upon the savages any respect for their ability to punish or restrain them.[26]

Scarcely had spring arrived when Washington reported that depredations had begun once more and that some Amer-ican citizens had been murdered at Taos. The regular military force had proven entirely inadequate and he had been obliged to summon a volunteer force which had ren-dered excellent service.[27] On May 30, there were ten more murders at the hands of the Apaches to report, and during the succeeding months the attacks were almost continuous. The need of a stronger cavalry force was urgently insisted upon.[28] But Congress was too much occupied with other problems to give adequate attention to the urgent needs of the distant territories.

The Indian Agency in Santa Fe. It was patent that the organization of the Indian Department, provided for in 1834, needed revision in view of the new problems which naturally resulted from the mere immensity of the recent territorial acquisition. But, since Congress failed to make the necessary changes, the President and the commissioner

25. *Ho. Ex. Doc. 5,* 31 Cong., 1 Sess., p. 105.
26. *Ho. Ex. Doc. I.,* 30 Cong., 2 Sess., p. 472.
27. *Ho. Ex. Doc. 5,* 31 Cong., 1 Sess., p. 106.
28. *Ibid.,* 108-10.

of Indian affairs were almost powerless until 1849 when it was determined, in consonance with the provisions of the Act of 1834 to move the Indian Agency from Council Bluffs to Santa Fe.[29]

James S. Calhoun was appointed first Indian agent for Santa Fe on April 7, 1849. His acquaintance with the region, although slight, and, more especially, political influence, were responsible for his appointment. ". . . he proved himself a thoroughly capable and honest official. Not a single scandal, not a single suspicion of peculation tarnished his record, and in his time, at least, that was a singularly rare experience in the United States Indian service."[30]

The office was to be no sinecure. No specific instructions could be given since practically nothing definite was known by the Indian Office of conditions in New Mexico.[31] Calhoun was instructed that he was depended upon to furnish.

> . . . such statistical and other information as will give a just and full understanding of every particular relating to them, embracing the names of the tribes, their location, the distance between the tribes, the probable extent of territory owned or

29. Calhoun, J. S., *Official Correspondence*, 1. "The Act of June 30, 1834 was 'An Act to Provide for the organization of the Department of Indian Affairs' and its 4th section reads as follows: '. . . And the President shall be and he is authorized, whenever he may judge it expedient, to discontinue any Indian Agency or to transfer the same, from the place or tribe designated by law, to such other place or tribe as the public service may require.' . . . Under existing law, the number of agencies was limited but that of sub-agencies unlimited. There were two Council Bluffs Indian establishments, a *sub-agency* on the Iowa side of the Missouri River, accommodating the 'united nations of Chippewas, Ottawa and Pottawatomie Indians' and an *agency* on the Nebraska side at Bellevue, accommodating the Otoes and Missourias, the Pawnees and the Omahas. Under the provisions of the Treaty of 1846 . . .' the United nation of Chippewa, Ottawa, and Pottawatomie Indians agreed 'to remove to their new homes on the Kansas River, within two years from the ratification of the treaty.' This discontinued the 'Council Bluffs Sub-Agency' and made it possible for the Indian Office to meet the new needs of the Southwest by reducing the 'Council Bluffs Agency' to a sub-Agency and, that done, completing the number of agencies by erecting one at Santa Fe." (Idem.)

30. Calhoun, J. S., *Official Correspondence*, xii-xiii, 3.

31. The Dept. of the Interior was created March 3, 1849, and the Office of Indian Affairs had been transferred as a bureau to it from the War Dept. Thomas Ewing whose family was interested in the Santa Fe trade was appointed first Secretary of the Department of the Interior (*Ibid.*, 9, 10).

claimed by each respectively and the tenure by which they hold or claim it; their manners and habits, their disposition and feelings towards the United States, Mexico and the whites generally and towards each other, whether hostile or otherwise; whether the several tribes speak different languages, and when different the apparent analogies between them, and also what laws and regulations for their government are necessary and how the law regulating trade and intercourse with the Indian tribes . . . will, if extended over that country, properly apply to the Indians there and to the trade and intercourse with them and what modification, if any, will be required to produce the greatest degree of efficiency.[32]

He was, moreover, instructed to use every possible means to obtain information regarding any Americans or Mexicans held captive, and if Mexican, whether their capture was prior or subsequent to the signing of the recent treaty. Evidently these last circumstances would affect the obligations of the United States.[33]

Calhoun undertook his duties at once, reaching Santa Fe July 22, 1849.[34] His voluminous correspondence reveals his intense interest in his new field of labor and his untiring efforts to have his suggestions acted upon by the federal government. In his first report he endeavored to give as accurate information regarding the Indian conditions as the short time he had been in New Mexico allowed. He advocated a conciliatory policy toward the Pueblo Indians whom he described as amicably disposed toward Americans, industrious and anxious to make progress. Toward the wild, roving tribes who had wrought havoc on all sides he advised sternness, in order to prove the power of the United States, and thus elicit respect, followed by generosity towards those who sought peace. He especially recommended an early consideration by Congress of the problem

---

32. Calhoun, *Correspondence*, 3.
33. *Ibid.*, 4.
34. *Ibid.*, 17.

presented by those tribes which had never learned to support themselves except by plunder.[35]

In the latter part of 1849 he summarized the suggestions he had made up to that date. He specifically recommended the appointment of agents at various points.

> Their presence is demanded by every principle of humanity, by every generous obligation of kindness, of protection, and of good government throughout this vast Territory. These agents . . . should be selected, not only with regard to their prudence and discretion, but with a view to the proper training of the Pueblo Indians in the efficient use of our arms. . . .
> By keeping up a proper line of communication between the pueblos and other places in this Territory, it will be no difficult matter to intercept roving bands of robbers, no matter what their color may be so soon as it is ascertained from what quarter they proceed; and that may be done unerringly by an examination of their trail.[36]

With the suggestions he sent a diagram to show the basis of his decision.[37] He suggested:

> 1st. The establishing of a full agency at Taos, or near that place, for the *Utahs,* and Pueblos of that neighborhood.
> 2nd. Also a full agency at and for Zunia, and the Navajoes.
> 3rd. A full agency at Socoro, a military post south of Albuquerque, now being established. The agent of this place to look after the Apaches and Comanches, and the pueblo of Isletta, north. Sub-agents should be sent to San Ildefonso, or near there; to Jemez, Laguna, and at the military post near El Paso.
> These agents and sub-agents are absolutely necessary to an economical administration of our Indian affairs in this Territory. It is my honest

35. *Ibid.,* 18-20.
36. *Ho. Ex. Doc.* 17, 31 Cong., 1 Sess., 223-4.
37. *Idem.*

opinion that for the ensuing year, at least, a sub-agent should be in every pueblo, the whole to be under the direction of a general superintendent . . .[38]

As time wore on, Calhoun began to realize more fully the magnitude of the task before him. But he felt himself equal to the situation if only adequate means were furnished by the federal government to meet the enormous expenditure necessarily incurred in New Mexico where prices were much higher than in the eastern states; if proper agencies were established; and if a strong military force were allowed for the territory or he were authorized to raise a volunteer force. The latter plan he considered the better.[39]

For three years he labored at a task which should have met with hearty coöperation, but, in reality, was almost ignored by Congress. His correspondence reveals, as nothing else could, the true state of affairs. On November 30, 1849, he wrote, "Matters in this territory are in a most deplorable condition, infinitely worse than you can imagine them, and which, without being an eye witness you cannot realize."[40] Traveling on the Santa Fe Trail was most hazardous; murders and depredations were of frequent occurrence; among those killed was a well known Mr. White whose wife and child were taken captive; the mail had been robbed; treaties were ignored; the government in the territory was inefficient; Colonel Munroe's refusal to keep Calhoun advised of his plans for suppressive measures by the military complicated affairs; American traders were exerting an evil influence; and Americans travelling through the Pueblo country had been guilty of outrageous conduct which had engendered a bitter feeling in these trustful people.[41]

---

38. *Ibid.*, 224.
39. *Ibid.*, 17, 57, 65, 104, 228, 255, 288.
40. *Ibid.*, 88.
41. Calhoun *Correspondence, passim.*

But Calhoun had more than complaints to offer. His suggestions were carefully planned to meet the exigencies of the situation. On January 15, 1850 he reported, "The trade and intercourse with the Apaches and Comanches by Mexicans, Americans, and Pueblo Indians, is rapidly increasing and until this is checked we cannot hope for the slightest improvement in our affairs.

1. Let the laws regulating trade, etc., be extended over these tribes at once.
2. Each tribe should have *fixed limits* assigned to them, and there compelled to remain, though the United States Government should have to support them for a time.
3. The laws of No. 1 should be extended over the Pueblos, and they divided in such a way as to give to each district an Agent and each pueblo for this year should have a sub-agent.
4. These Agents should have Ordnance and Ordnance Stores to be used as occasion may require.
5. It is my decided opinion it would be the best possible economy to send out two mounted regiments for service here—without them you cannot keep the Indians in the limits you may assign them, nor can you prevent an illicit trade and intercourse and the people of this territory must neither expect safety to their persons or property.

A few Indians ought to be called to Washington."[42]

The last suggestion was the one of the necessity of which Calhoun was evidently thoroughly convinced. He thought that by this means the Indians would be impressed with a true idea of the power of the United States for which they had little respect. He had reported in 1849 that ". . . the wild Indians of this country have been so much more successful in their robberies since General Kearny took possession of the country, they do not believe we have the power to chastise them." There are few so bold as to

---

42. *Ibid.*, 100.

travel alone ten miles from Santa Fe.[43] Thus the American population was decreasing. Many went to California or returned east.[44]

Some treaties with the Indians, notably those with the Navajoes and Utahs, had been entered into, but, like too many others, might just as well not have been drawn up. They did, however, give the two peoples an opportunity to come into close contact and thus revealed to the Americans characteristics of the Indians as well as the nature and extent of the territory. This information was found useful in determining the future policy.

Calhoun certainly used all the means at his command to comply with the terms of the Treaty of Guadalupe-Hidalgo. He had succeeded to a limited extent in accomplishing the provision regarding the liberation and return of captives. On at least three occasions he had such reports to make. On June 27, 1850, thirteen Mexican captives were confided to José M. Prieto at El Paso, five more were delivered in the same place on August 5, 1851, and later in the same month three others were being held awaiting the disposal of their government.[45]

But he repeatedly warned Washington that claims would undoubtedly be brought against the United States by Mexico for depredations committed along the border by the Indians who travelled with impunity from one side of the line to the other. To the argument that the expenses of the War Department must be cut down and therefore no more troops could be apportioned to New Mexico, he replied that a decisive show of strength would effectively put a stop to the possibility of plunder and the amount expended would be much less than the United States was making herself liable for.

By forcing the Indians to remain within prescribed bounds, the end would be gained. Besides preventing the

43. *Ibid.*, 31, 32.
44. *Sen. Ex. Doc.*, 1, 31 Cong., 2 Sess., p. 140; Calhoun, 28 *et seq.; Ho. Ex. Doc.* 5, 31 Cong., 1 Sess., 111-2.
45. Calhoun, *op. cit.*, 390, 401, 427.

depredations on the Mexican as well as American population, this line of action would render protection to the
Pueblo Indians who were becoming more and more dissatisfied with the conditions under American rule. Under both
Spain and Mexico they had been allowed to protect themselves from the inroads of the wild tribes, particularly the
Navajoes, by retaliatory raids. Now this was forbidden
them and they found themselves practically helpless.
Neither they nor the Mexicans could understand the propriety of the government at Washington refusing to allow
them to take vengeance on their aggressors when it was
evident that it could not protect them, unless it was the intention of this government to make good their losses from
its own treasury. They repeatedly demanded arms and
ammunition.[46]

Another source of grievance was the assumption of
power in the pueblos by the alcaldes who now found it
possible to rule in a most arbitrary fashion. Under the
Mexican domination they had exercised practically self-
government and were naturally opposed to its abrogation.
Furthermore their property rights were being questioned
by both American and Mexican claimants to land within
the pueblos.[47]

Calhoun soon realized that the intercourse of traders
with the Indians, particularly the Pueblos, required strict
and careful regulation. Their influence against the Indian
agency was constantly being manifested. Through the
traders the wild tribes obtained arms with which to nullify
the exertions of Calhoun. They worked on the fears of the
Pueblos by representing the weakness of the United States
and the certainty of the restoration of Mexican power which
would result in the extermination of those Indians who had
consented to the American rule. Their motive for this disgraceful course of action was the desire to exclude other
Americans from the Pueblo lands in which they were mak-

---

46. *Ibid.*, 31, 76.
47. *Ibid.*, 77.

ing a fortune by their bartering. The extent of the influence of the traders was manifested by their traveling with impunity through those regions in which the most hostile tribes dwelt.[48]

Definite but ineffectual efforts were made to regulate this traffic. On November 21, 1849, Calhoun was authorized by Governor Munroe to issue a notice regarding traders' licenses. Each applicant was obliged to give bond, not to exceed five thousand dollars, that he would not violate the general laws of the United States governing intercourse with the Indians and would not trade in implements of war. Licenses would authorize trading with a specific tribe and with no others. Permits for trade with the Apaches, Navajoes, and Utahs were for the time refused.[49]

To anyone conversant with the failure of the United States to enforce trade laws with the Indians throughout the entire west during these years, it is not surprising to find that these regulations of Calhoun were successfully evaded and the evil continued to as great an extent as before.

The very distance of New Mexico from the center of government and the difficulty of intercommunication between the two places increased the magnitude of problems of control. Much of the mail was lost and that which escaped the Indian raids, reached its destination only after a long delay. Thus often no authorization for a suggested course of action could be given to Calhoun whose powers were very limited, until the need of such action was passed.

The Indian Problem in Congress. By the close of the year 1849, practically nothing had been accomplished by the federal government except the establishment of an agency at Santa Fe. The good which this had been able to do could be attributed to the untiring efforts of the person who filled the office, rather than to any definite policy on the part of the United States, or, apparently, any lively interest in

---

48.   Calhoun, 51, 71; *Ho. Ex. Doc.* 17, 31 Cong., 1 Sess., *passim.*
49.   Calhoun, *op. cit.*, 105.

what was going on., Although partially due to ignorance of the true state of affairs, this indifference can also be traced to the absorbing nature of other problems with which the United States had to cope at the time and the successful blocking of legislation by the opponents of the administration.

The same was true in 1850 although at the close of the year Calhoun was appointed governor of the newly organized territory. This gave him more authority although disputes with the military power, represented by Sumner, were more pronounced than during the administration of Munroe who, though not always in sympathy with Calhoun's plans, did render effective assistance on many occasions.[50]

In January 1851, the commissioner of Indian affairs reported to Calhoun that with the exception of the report of the committee of Ways and Means recommending an appropriation of $36,000 for fulfilling the treaties of 1849 with the Navajoes and Utahs, no action had been taken by Congress in reference to Indian Affairs in New Mexico.[51]

Perhaps no peoples in the territory suffered more than the Pueblo Indians, yet Calhoun could report in 1849 that they were the only Indians in complete friendship with the government of the United States. He described them as "an industrious, agricultural and pastoral people living principally in villages . . . on both sides of the Rio Grande."[52]

In the "gold rush" to California many adventurers followed the road which passed by the Pueblo of Zuñi about two hundred miles from Santa Fé. These Indians were harassed by the Navajoes and Apaches but "what is shockingly discreditable to the American name, emigrants commit the greatest wrongs against these excellent Indians, by taking, in the name of the United States, such horses, mules, and sheep, and grain as they desire, carefully concealing their

---

50. *Ibid.*, *passim.*
51. *Ibid.*, 297.
52. *Ibid.*, 18.

true name, but assuming official authority and bearing."
The same, if not greater, wrongs were suffered by the Indians of Laguna.[53]

Calhoun repeatedly reported that neglect of the Pueblo
Indians, exposing them to attacks which they were not
allowed to repel with their own forces because they were
presumably under the protection of the United States, was
not only unjust but also impolitic. They would make willing
and useful allies in warfare with the roving bands of Indians. They could also supply the many necessary articles
of food if their industries were protected. "These people
can raise immense quantities of corn and wheat, and have
large herds of sheep and goats—the grazing for cattle generally is superior."[54]

Yet almost every letter from Calhoun recites the continuance of unrest and dissatisfaction. Having been promised protection, the Pueblos could not understand why it
was not accorded to them.

That the opinions of Calhoun were based on facts is
proven by the report of L. Lea, the Commissioner of Indian
Affairs in 1850 to the Secretary of the Interior.

> The ruinous condition of our Indian affairs in
> New Mexico demands the immediate attention of
> Congress. In no section of the country are prompt
> and efficient measures for restraining the Indians
> more imperiously required than in this territory,
> where an extraordinary state of things exists,
> which so long as it continues, will be a reproach to
> the government.
> There are over 30,000 Indians within its
> limits, the greater portion of which, having never
> been subjected to any salutary restraint are extremely wild and intractable. For many years
> they have been in the habit of making forays, not
> only within the Territory itself, but in the adjoining provinces of Mexico . . . Our citizens have suffered severely from their outrages within the last
> two years . . . Atrocities and aggressions are com-

53. *Ibid.*, 30-31, 45.
54. *Ibid.*, 40, 53

mitted not only upon our citizens but upon Pueblo Indians. . . . Before the country came into our possession, they were in the habit of repairing the injuries they sustained by retaliation and reprisals upon their enemies; but from this they are required to desist; and thus the duty is more strongly imposed upon us of affording them adequate protection. The interference of the government is required also to secure them against violations of their rights of persons and property by unprincipled white men, from whose cupidity and lawlessness they are continually subject to grievous annoyance and oppression.

. . . It is believed that by pursuing a wise and liberal policy toward them . . . they will in a few years be fitted to become citizens; and being industrious, moral, and exemplary, in their habits will constitute a valuable portion of the population of the territory.[55]

On February 27, 1851, an appropriation was made for four Indian agents for New Mexico and one for Utah;[56] but little more was done by the federal government.

The responsibility for this inertia cannot be laid to the charge of the administration. The conditions on the frontier formed a vital part of President Fillmore's message of December 1850. The President called the attention of Congress to the deplorable state of affairs and reminded the members of our treaty obligations to Mexico which were not being fulfilled.[57]

Any effort to obtain an appropriation for the proper management of the Indians which meant an increase in the army brought forth discussions on the responsibility for the Mexican War or other party issues; and the Committee on Ways and Means was inclined to cut down the estimates sent in by the War Department.

Criticism of the expense of maintaining the army considered so extravagant in peace times was heard on all sides.

55. *Sen. Ex. Doc.* I, 31 Cong., 2 Sess., p. 42.
56. *Rippy, op. cit.,* 118.
57. Richardson, *Messages and Papers of the President* V, 87.

The answer was always the same. We had taken the burden on ourselves by the treaty and moreover, less would be required to convince the Indians of the power of the United States than would later be necessary to subdue them when a real war, which could be expected daily, should break out.[58] Some would even return the newly acquired land to Mexico and even give her a few millions to take it back.[59] Later it was solemnly suggested by the Secretary of War that all the land be bought from the inhabitants and they be given land elsewhere since it was not from any viewpoint worth the money which was being spent. The Indians could then be left in undisputed possession.[60]

Still nothing decisive was done and conditions in New Mexico daily became worse. On July 9, 1851, Governor Calhoun received a memorial from the people of Santa Fé setting forth the lamentable state of the country since the American occupation. In order to show the unqualified necessity of raising a volunteer force composed of the people of New Mexico to protect their own lives and property, the statement was made

> . . . at the present time New Mexico does not possess one tenth of the property she owned in the previous years; it has been swept away as by an impetuous torrent, our prosperity has been converted into misfortune and the present miserable condition of New Mexico is the fatal result of the misfortune which has taken place paralyzing every branch of industry to the greatest degree and being the cause of continued murders and the taking of nearly all the property owned in New Mexico.[61]

Finally in August 1852, $20,000 were appropriated for general Indian service in New Mexico and the general appropriation bill set aside $65,000 for the segregation of the Indians according to the early suggestions of Calhoun.

---

58. *Cong. Globe*, 31 Cong., 2 Sess., 689, 721 *et. seq.*
59. *Cong. Globe*, 30 Cong., 1 Sess., 1052-1063.
60. *Cong. Globe, App.* 32 Cong., 2 Sess., 103 *et seq.*
61. Calhoun, *op. cit.*, 386.

But this was a paltry sum in view of the expense of patrolling the frontier and though conditions were somewhat improved in New Mexico during the next year, the Indians were causing greater havoc than ever on the Mexican side of the boundary.[62]

The Indian agents who had been appointed made considerable effort to meet the obligations of the treaty of Guadalupe-Hidalgo. Before December 30, 1853, when the Gadsden Treaty changed the responsibility completely, four important Indian treaties were made, three of which were ratified by Congress. Each provided that the Indians should deliver up Mexican prisoners. The treaty with the Gila Apaches, even went so far as to pledge the Indians in future to desist from making hostile or predatory incursions into Mexico. It is well known that these Indians had numerous Mexican prisoners and it is safe to assume that after the signing of the treaty these were returned to their homes. Something, then, had been accomplished by the agents notwithstanding the difficuty of their task.[63]

The Indian Policy of Mexico. There is no foundation in fact for the assumption that Mexico made no attempts to defend herself from the Indians during this time, and refused to coöperate with the efforts, such as they were, of the United States.[64]

Immediately after the treaty of Guadalupe-Hidalgo, the northern frontier was marked out into three divisions, the Frontier of the East, the Frontier of Chihuahua, and the Frontier of the West. Among these eighteen colonies were distributed. Generous offers were made to those who would second the efforts of the Government to make settlements on the boundary. The land around each colony, after being improved at government expense, was to be assigned to the soldiers for cultivation. During his terms of service, the soldier, recruited by voluntary enlistment for

62. Rippy, *op. cit.*, 118, 135.
63. Calhoun, *op. cit.*, 314-16 ; Rippy 126-7.
64. This account of the efforts made by Mexico to protect herself is based on Rippy, J. F., *Relations of the United States and Mexico, 1848-1860*, 135-151.

a term of six years, was to share the fruits of the soil, and at the expiration of his term was to receive a bounty of ten pesos and the allotment of land which he had been cultivating. Provision was also made for civilian settlers around each colony which, on reaching a certain population, was to be given a civil government.

In the course of the next four years all the colonies were set up either permanently or temporarily. Soldiers had been recruited, and by treaties in 1850 and 1852 with peaceful Seminoles and Muskogees, they had been permitted to settle in the vicinity of the colonies of the East and Chihuahua; in 1851 reduced Sierra Gorda Indians were sent to increase the frontier forces.

The towns on the frontier exposed to the Indian raids formed leagues for common defense, and private individuals contributed to war and ransom funds. Finally the frontier states of Nuevo Leon, Chihuahua, Zacatecas, Tamaulipas, and San Luis Potosi (1851) began plans for union for the purpose of self-defense.

That these measures were ineffective was due to the internal dissensions in Mexico, "the chaotic state of the national funds, the poverty of the frontier states, epidemics of cholera and fever, the quest for gold which drew a large number of Sonorans annually to California, and lastly by the filibusterers who, beginning their raids in 1851, kept the whole northern frontier in almost constant agitation."[65]

Numerous complaints were made by Mexico on account of the failure of the United States to fulfill the obligations imposed by Article XI of the Treaty of Guadalupe-Hidalgo. In March 1850, De la Rosa, the Mexican Minister at Washington, represented that the only advantage which could "compensate Mexico for the many sacrifices" which the late treaty "rendered necessary" was the exact fulfillment of the stipulations in regard to the Indians. Early in January, 1852, the Mexican Minister of Relations, Ramirez, demanded that "in virtue of this obligation—contracted and

---

65. *Idem.*

not fulfilled—means should be devised to indemnify Mexico for the fatal consequences" which had resulted.

The United States Government held that it was not liable for damages inflicted by the Indians but that it was only obliged to exact the same satisfaction from the savages for raids into Mexico as if these had been against the United States. Reports that Mexico was preparing to present heavy claims and that speculators were buying up these claims caused efforts to be made to obtain release from the Article which it was now seen to be practically impossible to fulfill. The complete story of the efforts made by the United States to obtain this release has never been told, but it is known that the attempts made during the latter part of 1851 to gain this end by a payment of some six or seven million dollars were failures.

The border Indian problem, then, served as one of the many incentives to the United States to endeavor to bring about a satisfactory adjustment of the strained relations between herself and Mexico. That this was achieved through the Gadsden Treaty has already been noted. The greatest gain to the United States was the abrogation of Article XI of the former treaty. The Indian situation thereby lost its international character but did not cease to be one of the most difficult problems with which the United States was obliged to cope in the Southwest. The account of how satisfactory control was finally effected belongs to the later history of the United States.

CHAPTER VI

THE ESTABLISHMENT OF CIVIL GOVERNMENT

In New Mexico, as in the other districts acquired by the terms of the Treaty of Guadalupe Hidalgo, the question of government was of vital importance. General Kearny had established a full territorial organization, appointing civil officers and a complete system of courts, and had assumed that thenceforth the inhabitants of the country were citizens of the United States.

Official Disapproval of the Kearny Code. On receipt of a copy of the laws known as the Kearny Code, the secretary of war, Marcy, instructed by the president, wrote to Kearny, January 11, 1847. He mildly rebuked him for his action, remarking that the political rights conferred upon the people could be acquired only by the action of congress and that, in so far as the code of laws attempted to confer these rights, it was not approved by the president and was not to be carried into effect. Kearny was upheld in so far as he had set up a civil government in the conquered land, for it was recognized that this was necessary for the preservation of good order.[1]

When, in 1846, the house of representatives asked information from the president regarding the establishment of civil government in territory belonging to Mexico, Polk replied in December, that while the establishment of territorial government by Kearny was not approved or recognized by him, yet there could be no doubt that any excessive exercise of civil power by the officers in the conquered provinces was not due to arrogance but rather the result of an effort to spread the blessings of peace with the least possible delay.[2]

---

1. Sec. of War Marcy, to Brig. Gen. S. W. Kearny, January 11, 1847. *Ho. Ex. Doc. 60*, 30 Cong., 1 Sess., p. 179.

One cannot fail to perceive that the attacks in congress before and after the reception of the message were inspired by political opposition rather than by any consuming interest in the legality of the point at issue. They brought out, however, interesting views on the status of inhabitants of conquered territories and the authority of the United States government therein.[3] Notwithstanding the refusal of those in authority to ratify fully the acts of Kearny, the civil government as set up by him continued to perform its functions, but its effectiveness cannot be decided upon since practically nothing is recorded of its actual operations in 1846-1847. This may raise the question whether or not there was anything to record.[4]

Military Rule in New Mexico. After the revolt of 1846-7, the power of the civil authorities was almost completely subordinated to that of the military. This was, beyond doubt, in consonance with the orders to Kearny, but was resented by the people who had assumed that the civil code set up by Kearny had been fully approved by the president.[5]

That this supremacy of the military power was in full accord with the will of the administration was strikingly evidenced soon after it was enforced. On the death of Governor Bent in January 1847, Secretary Vigil became acting governor. In his report to the president he emphatically

2. *Appendix, Cong. Globe,* 30 Cong., 1 Sess., p. 934.

3. *Cong. Globe,* 30 Cong., 2 Sess., In a case growing out of the Mexican War, Chief Justice Taney, two years later, delivered a statement which ably sums up judicial decision in this question. "The relation in which the conquered territory stood to the United States while it was occupied by their arms did not depend on the laws of nations but upon our own constitution and acts of Congress . . . The inhabitants were still foreigners and enemies, and owed to the United States nothing more than the submission and obedience, sometimes called temporary allegiance, which is due from a conquered enemy when he surrenders to a force which he is unable to resist. (Fleming vs. Page, 9 How., 615 *et seq.,* as cited in D. Y. Thomas, *A History of Military Government in Newly Acquired Territory of the United States,* 112.)

4. Bancroft, *Arizona and New Mexico,* 428.

5. Twitchell, R. E., *The Military Occupation of the Territory of New Mexico,* 147. Read states that this assumption of power by Colonel Price caused the people to be divided into two factions, the one supporting, the other opposing the military rule. (*History of New Mexico,* 453.)

stated that necessity alone had induced him to take upon himself the duties and responsibilities of the position since he felt that his own office was too arduous for him to endeavor to do anything more. He requested the president to replace him as soon as possible and suggested for the office Ceran St. Vrain "a native of Missouri, though an occasional resident of this territory for many years back." He gave assurance that this appointment would meet with the unanimous approval of the people.[6]

Marcy, secretary of war, writing to Price the following June (1847) replied that the filling of the office of governor was the function of the senior military officer to whom the civil officer was subordinate and therefore it rested with him to appoint someone to this position, should Vigil still wish to retire.[7] Vigil, who was then appointed governor by General Price in December, continued to hold office nominally until October 1848.[8]

The Convention of 1847. Meanwhile, in accordance with the provisions of the Kearny Code, the first legislature of New Mexico had been elected and had held a regular session beginning on December 6, 1847.[9] This was organized by the election of Don Antonio Sandoval as speaker of the legislative council and Captain W. Z. Angney the speaker of the house of representatives. Among the ten acts passed were two of special interest as indicating the desires of the people. One provided for the establishment of a university with the funds for its support; the other called for a convention of delegates to meet in the city of Santa Fé in February 1848. Governor Vigil and General Price both gave their approval to the acts.[10]

Notwithstanding this show of civil power, the syn-

---

6. *Ho. Ex. Doc.*, 70, 30 Cong., 1 Sess., pp. 19-20.
7. *Ibid.*, p. 32.
8. Bancroft, *op. cit.*, 442.
9. Prince, L. B., *New Mexico's Struggle for Statehood*, 7.
10. Pamphlet of Laws. Session 1847 in library of F. Springer, Las Vegas, New Mexico, as cited in R. E. Twitchell, *The Military Occupation of New Mexico*, 151. *Legislative Manual*, 180-181.

chronous acts of Price reveal the eminently military character of the government. Having been convinced that a territorial secretary, a United States district attorney, and a United States marshal were unnecessary, he abolished these offices by special order. He also decreed that a six per cent ad valorem duty should be levied on all merchandise introduced into the Territory. The territorial treasurer was named collector of customs on such imports, and sub-collectorships were established at Taos, San Miguel and Valencia. Under a license of $2,000 a year, licensed gambling houses were established.[11]

These laws were in consonance with the order issued in March 1847 by President Polk, whereby military and naval commanders were instructed "to levy and collect a military contribution upon all vessels and merchandise which might enter any of the ports of Mexico in our military occupation, and to apply such contributions towards defraying the expenses of the war." Justification for this law was found in the fact that previous to the war, the revenue derived from import duties went into the Mexican treasury, and that it was within the competence of the United States to close the ports or regulate the tariff. She chose the latter course.[12]

It was easier to make such laws than to enforce them. Indignation meetings were held for the purpose of protesting against providing in this way for revenue for the payment of the expenses of the government. The argument was put forth that in imposing this duty undue discrimination was being exerted against one section of the country. Complaints reached Washington, and, in October, the federal government ordered a refund of all duties collected on goods brought into the Territory from the United States subsequent to the thirtieth of May.[13]

---

11. Orders No. 10, General Price, War. Rec. Wash. D. C., Reports of General Sterling Price as cited in R. E. Twitchell, *The Military Occupation of New Mexico*, 151.

12. *Cong. Globe*, 30 Cong., 1 Sess., 339.

13. Twitchell, R. E., *Leading Facts of New Mexican History* II, 268; *Cong. Globe*, 30 Cong., 1 Sess., 1847, pp. 284-339.

Doubtless this method of raising money seemed to Price the only solution of a pressing difficulty. Officers had been appointed, according to the provisions of the Kearny Code, and there was no appropriation made for the payment of their salaries. These salaries were for the most part unpaid when New Mexico was finally made a territory.[14]

By the ratification of the treaty with Mexico, all the people of New Mexico were constituted citizens of the United States except those who formally preferred to retain their Mexican citizenship. The manifestation of such desire was to be made within one year.[15]

Desire of Polk to Have Territorial Government Established. In transmitting the treaty to congress, President Polk suggested that immediate attention be given to the organization of the newly acquired provinces:

> The immediate establishment of territorial government and the extension of our laws over these valuable possessions are deemed to be not only important, but indispensable to preserve order, and the due administration of justice within their limits, to afford protection to the inhabitants, and to facilitate the development of the vast resources and wealth which their acquisition has added to our country.[16]

---

14. Twitchell, R. E., *Leading Facts of New Mexican History* II, 268. On May 3, 1852, the secretary of war in answer to a resolution of the senate calling for information in relation to civil officers employed in the territory of New Mexico while under military government reported $31,562.37 due on March 31, 1851. Governor Calhoun wrote, "I cannot too strongly urge the government of the United States to provide for the immediate payment of these claims, not only because justice to the claimants named demands it, but for the additional reason that $12,698.64 is due to the territorial treasury . . . and there is not one dollar in the territorial treasury and the collection of taxes is resisted with no prospect of an early adjustment of the question involved." (*Sen. Ex. Doc. 71,* 32 Cong., 1 Sess., pp. 1-3.)

15. Treaty of Guadalupe-Hidalgo Act VIII and IX. *Ho. Ex. Doc. 69,* 30 Cong. 1 Sess., pp. 17-18. According to correspondence between Secretary Vigil and Don Ramón Ortiz, who went from Mexico to New Mexico for the purpose of assisting those who wished to take advantage of the opportunity to return to Mexico and thus retain their Mexican citizenship, there were many who desired to emigrate. Vigil opposed the movement and Ortiz was constrained to return to Mexico. (Pino, *Noticias Históricas y Estadísticas,* (Escudero ed. 1849) 92-98.)

16. Mess. of Pres. J. K. Polk, July 6, 1848. *Ho. Ex. Doc. 69,* 30 Cong., 1 Sess.

The Polk administration had been steadily declining in popularity. Each clause of the message gave material for violent partisan debate. The result was that no measures of organization were framed during the session.[17]

The properly qualified body had failed to legislate in the matter, and as late as August 1848, the war department had apparently issued no orders defining the status of affairs in New Mexico.[18]

Suggestion of Senator Benton to New Mexico. Senator Thomas H. Benton of Missouri had taken it upon himself to represent the interests of New Mexico in congress. In September, 1848, he wrote to the people of California and New Mexico giving them his advice as to the wisest course for them to pursue until they were fully admitted to citizenship. He advised them to meet in convention and provide a government for themselves since it was not probable that congress would legislate for them for some time.[19]

Polk thought that Benton was thus secretly planning to make his son-in-law, Frémont, governor of California. The cabinet agreed with Polk in the wisdom of sending a a message to the people, warning them that such action would not be legal and that it would be to their best interests to continue in obedience to the *de facto* temporary government.[20]

Convention of 1848. Address to Congress. Nevertheless the suggestion of Senator Benton was acted upon. Under the proclamation of Governor Vigil a convention was assembled, October 11, 1848, with Antonio José Martinez as president. The most significant accomplishment was the formulation of a petition to congress. Because of the importance attached in Washington to a number of the clauses, it seems necessary to cite it in full:

---

17. See *App. Cong. Globe*, 30 Cong., 1 Sess., p. 880 *et seq.*
18. Thomas, D. Y., *A History of Military Government in Newly Acquired Territory of the United States*, 130.
19. Niles, 74, pp. 244-5.
20. Polk, *Diary*, Sept. 30, Oct. 3, 1848.

We the people of New Mexico respectfully petition Congress for the speedy organization, by law, of a territorial government for us.

We respectfully petition Congress to grant us a government purely civil in its character.

We respectfully represent that the organic and statute laws promulgated by the authority of the United States, September 22, 1846, for the temporary civil government of New Mexico (a copy of which is dispatched) with some few alterations would be acceptable to us.

We desire the following offices to be filled by appointment of the President of the United States, by and with the advice and consent of the Senate: the Governor, Secretary of State, United States Marshal, United States District Attorney, and Judges.

We desire to have all the usual rights of appeal from the courts of this Territory to the Supreme Court of the United States.

We respectfully but firmly protest against the dismemberment of our territory in favor of Texas or for any cause.

We do not desire to have domestic slavery within our borders; and until the time shall arrive for our admission into the Union as a State, we desire to be protected by Congress against their introduction among us.

We desire a local Legislature, such as is prescribed in the Laws of New Mexico, September 22, 1846, subject to the usual acts of Congress.

We desire that our interests may be represented by a delegate, who is to be entitled to have a seat upon the floor of the Congress of the United States.

In consideration of the fact that New Mexico contains from seventy-five thousand to one hundred thousand souls, we believe that we have made no unreasonable request, and we confidently rely upon Congress to provide for us laws as liberal as any enjoyed by any of the Territories.[21]

---

21. *Cong. Globe,* 30 Cong., 2 Sess., p. 33. For signatures see Ritch, W. G., *Legislative Blue Book of the Territory of New Mexico,* 100.

Opposition in Congress. Copies of the petition were forwarded to Senators Benton of Missouri and Clayton of Delaware. The former presented it in the senate on December 13, 1848. It was as a spark cast into a highly inflammable mass. The fires of sectional strife that had been smouldering ever since the day that the president had asked for an appropriation of $2,000,000 for the prosecution of the war, and the Wilmot Proviso was suggested, burst forth in seemingly unquenchable vigor. This appeared to be a direct challenge to the southern interests.

Mr. Calhoun of South Carolina denounced the petition as not only not respectful but "most insolent." In it he saw an unmistakable attempt to limit the power of the south; an attack by the conquered on the very people who had conquered them. He argued that the new territory belonged to the southern states as well as to the northern since the common treasury and southern lives had been given for the cause.

The claim of Texas to land west of the Rio Grande still further complicated matters. Mr. Rush of Texas protested against the attempt to establish a distinct government in what was unquestionably a part of Texas, although he advocated the organization of the remainder.[22]

After continued discussion in regard to the impertinence and disrespect of the petition, it was finally objected by one of the senators, Mr. Foote, that there was no proof that any convention had actually been held and that the petition purporting to come from the people of New Mexico, was, in reality, the work of only a negligible faction. He asserted that such an important event would, without doubt, have found a prominent place in the newspapers and their silence about the matter cast grave doubt upon it. Thus did the slave interests endeavor to prevent the impression gaining ground that New Mexico itself was opposed to slavery.

Finally the question was referred to a committee on

22. *Cong. Globe.*, 30 Cong.. 2 Sess., p. 33. The question of the Texas boundary will be treated more fully in the following chapter.

territories and nothing further was done in that session of congress.[23]

Convention of 1849. The lack of regularly organized government was keenly felt in New Mexico. In September 1849, Lieutenant Colonel Beall, acting as governor during the absence of Colonel Washington who had succeeded Price, issued a proclamation calling for the election of delegates to another convention to consider a plan for civil government. The convention elected Hugh N. Smith as a delegate to congress. In the resolutions drawn up on this occasion no protest was made against slavery or Texan encroachments. The delegate was instructed to use his endeavors to obtain a territorial rather than a state form of government taking as a model for the former the act constituting Minnesota a territory, but if he saw that only a state government could be obtained he should use the constitution of Missouri as a type.[24] In case a state governmen were insisted upon by the United States, the appointed delegate was instructed, among other things, that since the public lands were comparatively worthless and the grant of 500,000 acres was impracticable, to insist on an equivalent in money or that the United States pay annually $30,000 for ten years for the purpose of sustaining the government. He was also to stipulate that $100,000 be donated in lieu of the public buildings which congress would have been obliged to erect if a territorial government had been established. The interest in the advancement of learning is indicated by the provision that liberal grants be made for the establishment of colleges and common schools and for suitable institutions for the development of the arts and sciences.[25]

The difficulties under which the people were suffering were set forth in no ambiguous language. In the memorial to congress we read:

---

23. *Cong. Globe.*, 30 Cong., 2 Sess., p. 35-37 (Dec. 19, 1848). The question of the organization of New Mexico was intimately bound up with that of Oregon and California but it is impossible to develop these interesting topics here.

24. *Ho. Mis., Doc. 39*, 31 Cong., 1 Sess., 1-11.

25. *Ibid.*

. . . Whereas for the last three years, we have suffered under the paralyzing effects of a government undefined and doubtful in its character; inefficient to protect the rights of the people, or to discharge the high and absolute duty of every government, the enforcement and regular administration of its own laws, in consequence of which industry and enterprise are paralyzed and discontent and confusion prevail throughout the land; the want of proper protection against the various barbarous tribes of Indians that surround us on every side, has prevented the extension of settlements upon our valuable public domain and rendered utterly futile every attempt to explore or develop the great resources of the territory . . . we have neither the means nor any adopted plan by government for the education of the rising generation; in fine with a government temporary, doubtful, uncertain and inefficient in character and in operation, surrounded and despoiled by barbarous foes, ruin appears inevitable before us, unless speedy and effectual protection be extended to us by the Congress of the United States.[26]

Governor Washington did not officially recognize the acts of this convention. Nevertheless, Smith started for Washington, but by a vote of 92 to 86 the house, after a long discussion, refused to admit him as a delegate.[27]

The committee on elections reported that although New Mexico while a part of Mexico possessed a complete political organization, it could not be claimed that this organization continued after the cession of the territory to the United States. Though it was doubtless true that New Mexico was suffering difficulties and embarrassment because of the lack of civil government, this could not be taken into consideration in deciding on the admission of the delegate. The admission of Mr. Smith could not ameliorate these difficulties and all precedent was against such a step. In every case in which a delegate from a territory was admitted to

---

26. *Ibid.* Quoted in Clay's speech in senate, Feb. 5, 1850. *App. Cong. Globe,* 31 Cong., 1 Sess., 119.

27. *House Report No. 22,* 31 Cong., 1 Sess., v. II.

the congress of the United States he had been elected according to laws enacted by congress and from a government subordinate to and emanating from the constitution and laws of the United States. As a government, New Mexico was unknown to the laws of the United States. The admission of the delegate would be a *quasi* recognition of New Mexico as an organized government. A decisive element in the matter was the claim of Texas to the eastern bank of the Rio Grande. The admission of a delegate from a region thus under the claim of a region already represented would be too anomalous to need any further discussion. The minority report makes clear that the Texan claim was uppermost in the thoughts of the members of the committee which decided against the delegate from New Mexico.[28]

Both in the house and in the senate the controversy over the new territory, particularly in reference to the introduction of slavery, continued with ever increasing bitterness and the solution of the difficulties seemed farther away each day.

Attempt to form a State Government. President Taylor encouraged the application for admission into the Union as a state,[29] and even before Smith had failed to secure for New Mexico the status of territory an attempt was made in New Mexico for the formation of state government. This was mainly due to the efforts of James S. Calhoun who, in 1849, was sent to New Mexico as Indian agent. It became known that he had semi-official instructions to favor the organization of state government. The resulting agitation at first bore little fruit, but the following summer the people became definitely divided into a state and a territorial party. Each issued its manifestos and for a time party strife ran high.

In the early part of 1850 Colonel McCall joined his regiment in New Mexico. He made it clear to the people that congress would not grant a territorial government and

28. *Ho. Rep. 220*, 31 Cong., 1 Sess., II, *passim.*
29. Richardson, *Messages and Papers of the Presidents*, V, p. 27.

that President Taylor was determined that New Mexico should be erected into a state in order definitely to settle the question of slavery therein and that of the boundary of Texas.[30] This news, together with a threatened attack from without, put an end to internal dissension. A commission arrived from Texas claiming jurisdiction over eastern New Mexico.[31] The parties forgot their differences and united to organize as a state. Colonel Monroe, then military governor, in response to a formal request of the people, on April 23, 1850, issued a call for the election of delegates to a convention to be summoned for the purpose and to urge upon congress her admission to the Union.[32]

The convention, ninety per cent of whose members were Mexicans, met at Santa Fé on the fifteenth of May. After a session of ten days a constitution was formulated. The boundaries of New Mexico, embracing the disputed area, were definitely stated.[33] Slavery was prohibited and freedom of religion, speech, and of the press guaranteed. Trial by jury was ordered except in civil cases involving less than fifty dollars in which case the legislature was authorized to provide for summary trial. Annual meeting of the legislature was ordered, the representatives holding office for two years, the senators for four. The state was divided into three judicial districts. The counties of Bernalillo and Valencia were to compose the southern circuit; the counties of Santa Ana, Santa Fé, and San Miguel, the central circuit; and the counties of Taos and Rio Arriba the northern circuit. This was to be effective only until the first census was taken after which the state was to be divided into four judicial districts. The laws were to be revised every five years.

The first session of the first legislature was to be held at the recognized capital, Santa Fé, on the first day of July, 1850.

30. Davis, *El Gringo*, 111-2; Bancroft, *op. cit.*, 446. Prince, *The Struggle for Statehood*, 17-18.
31. Bancroft, *op. cit.*, 454-5; Read, *Illustrated History of New Mexico*, 456.
32. *Sen. Ex. Doc. 60*, 31 Cong., 1 Sess., p. 1-3.
33. *Sen. Ex. Doc. 74*, 31 Cong., 1 Sess. V. XIX.

Education was again provided for in the article:

The Legislature shall at as early a day as practicable, establish free schools throughout the State, and shall furnish means for their support by taxation; and it shall be the duty of the legislature to set apart not less than one-twelfth of the annual revenue of the State derived from taxation as a perpetual fund, which fund shall be appropriated to the support of free public schools; and no law shall be made diverting said fund to any other use.[34]

By order of the military governor, the instrument was submitted to the people for ratification and a vote cast for governor, lieutenant governor, representative to congress, and for senators and representatives to a state legislature. It was explicitly stated that those so elected were to hold office only on condition that the constitution receive the approval of the people and the state be admitted into the Union. Previous to admission only such acts were to be considered valid as were necessary for the preparation of the constitution in final form and its presentation to congress. The form of government then in existence was declared to be the only legal one until such time as congress organized some other form.[35]

The constitution was adopted with practically unanimous consent.[36] Henry Connelly, a prominent trader on the Santa Fé trail, and Manuel Alvarez, for many years United States consul at Santa Fé, were elected to the offices of governor and lieutenant-governor respectively, and Wm. S. Messervy was chosen as representative to congress.[37]

Little attention was paid to Governor Munroe's limiting provisions. The legislature, meeting in the early part of July, continued in session over a week. Francis A. Cunningham and Richard H. Weightman were elected United States senators, and general legislation was enacted. It was evi-

34. *Sen. Ex. Doc. 74*, 31 Cong., 1 Sess., Vol. XIV.
35. *Sen. Ex. Doc. I*, 31 Cong., 2 Sess., 91-94.
36. 6,771 votes for and 39 votes against. *Sen. Ex. Doc. 74*, 31 Cong., 1 Sess., 2.
37. *Sen. Ex. Doc. 26*, 31 Cong., 2 Sess., p. 10; Ritch, *Legislative Blue Book*, 100.

dent that the state would consider itself organized without waiting for any action from congress.

Munroe found himself in a difficult position. He protested against the proceedings as extra-legal. This led to a controversy between him and the acting governor Alvarez. The latter held that the military governor had no authority in this matter since his civil power surely could not be greater than that of the president "and that the President had never pretended to have the power to make a government for New Mexico or insist on the old one; that the President's instructions, and all others from Washington, simply advised temporary submission to the old government as existing by presumed consent of the people. That consent had been withdrawn and a new government organized, which must be recognized until Congress should refuse to sanction it."[38] For a time it seemed that there would be an armed conflict between the two factions but by mutual compromises this was avoided.

The Compromise of 1850; New Mexico a Territory of the United States. While New Mexico was thus endeavoring to solve her difficulties, the halls of congress were resounding with the greatest speeches in the annals of our history. It was universally felt that the new western territories could no longer be left in their unorganized condition, yet, every mention of the question brought forth violent debate from the two opposing sections. Slavery had without a doubt become a paramount issue. The prophetic words of J. E. Brady of Pennsylvania as early as 1848 had been verified. "Before this war we were divided as parties, it is true, but that division was a division of opinion upon questions of policy affecting each and every part of this confederacy. Now sir, I fear we shall ere long be divided into northern and southern parties, the consequences of which no man can foresee." [39]

---

38. *Sen. Ex. Dos. 1,* pt. II, 31 Cong., 2 Sess., pp. 96-106.
39. Speech of J. E. Brady in the house, June 27, 1848. *Cong. Globe App.* 30 Cong., 1 Sess., p. 790.

One plan after another had been suggested by means of which it was hoped that the threatened severing of the nation might be averted. As early as 1848 Polk had proposed, among other plans, the extension of the Missouri Compromise line to the Pacific.[40] This met with little or no consideration and was dropped. Others endeavored to show that the question of slavery was beside the point; that nature herself together with long established custom had made the institution impossible in the new territories. In impassioned language Clay cried out, "What do you want? you who reside in the free states. . . . You have got more than a thousand Wilmot provisos. You have nature upon your side—facts upon your side and this truth staring you in the face, that there is no slavery in those territories." [41] Webster took the same stand and asserted that he "would not be at pains to reaffirm an ordinance of nature or reënact the will of God."

The great debate in which figured the famous orators, Webster, Clay, Calhoun, Seward, and others of lesser note, belongs properly to the history of the United States as a whole and can only be referred to here.[42] Although Clay's Compromise Bill of 1850 was apparently defeated, it was actually accepted in all its main provisions. A compromise, it but postponed a definite settlement of the difficulties which ultimately led to such dire results. But, for the time, strife seemed to be quelled. One section of the Compromise provided for the organization of territorial governments in the new provinces with no regulation in regard to slavery. The question was to be settled by each for itself.

The Act which established territorial government in New Mexico is entitled "An act proposing to the State of Texas the Establishment of her Northern and Western boundaries, the Relinquishment by the said State of all ter-

---

40. Speech of President Polk, 1848. Richardson, *Messages and Papers.*
41. Speech of Clay in senate, Feb. 5, 1850. *App. Cong. Globe,* 31 Cong., 1 Sess., pp. 118-119.
42. See *Cong. Globe,* 31 Cong., 1 Sess., *part I and Appendix, passim.*

ritory claimed by her exterior to said boundaries, and of all of her claims upon the United States, and to establish a Territorial Government of New Mexico." [43]

While even the title seems to subordinate New Mexican to Texas problems, the Act fully provided for the setting up of a complete territorial government. There was scarcely a provision which would differentiate this Act from those of a similar nature. It was proclaimed in force on December 13, 1850, by President Fillmore.

Thus was the career of the new state of New Mexico summarily ended. William S. Messervy was admitted to congress as a delegate from the territory instead of a representative of the state; the two senators elect found themselves bearing titles without office. James S. Calhoun was appointed first governor of the territory and the machinery of territorial government was put into operation in March 1851.[44] The years of uncertainty were over. New Mexican interests were those of the United States.

---

43. Territory of New Mexico, *Legislative Manual*, 34.
44. Prince, *New Mexico's Struggle for Statehood*, 22.

CHAPTER VII

THE DETERMINATION OF BOUNDARIES

Inseparably connected with the question of the organization of the government of the newly acquired district of New Mexico was the problem of determining the real limits of the region. While self-interest on the part of various factions, notably the Texans, the Mormons, and those determined on either the extension or the destruction of the slave power of the south, cast apparent or real doubt on the true boundaries, there was in reality foundation for the uncertainty. For a proper understanding of the situation it is necessary to review, in at least a cursory manner, the history of the gradual delimitation of New Mexico.

Boundaries during the Spanish Period. As Spain thrust her exploratory or colonizing enterprises farther and farther north, one of her chief motives was to insure control of one more section of the vast expanse of the Americas which she claimed as her own dominion. As new provinces were formed it was but natural that the northern boundaries should be designated in very vague terms. "The many barbarous nations or the gentile Indians generally formed this limit." [1] The authorities of New Spain drew up in a general way the limits on the south, west, and east since the contiguous provinces were necessarily differentiated; but time alone would determine the northern extent. When it became evident that a territory was too extensive for efficient control from one centre, districts were cut off and new nuclei formed. Thus Nueva Vizcaya was contracted by the formation of the province of New Mexico. [2]

1. Cox, I. J., "The Southwest Boundary of Texas," in *Tex. Hist. Assoc. Quart.*, VI, 84.
2. *Loc. Cit.*

On the east, New Mexico extended to the boundary of Florida, wherever that might be; on the west to the "South Sea" or Pacific Ocean; and no one knew how far north. The establishment of Louisiana and later of California reduced it to within commensurate bounds on the east and west, but even at the time of the Louisiana Purchase, 1803, there was still ground for disagreement in regard to its actual extent.[3]

When, in 1811, an order issued in 1804 by the king of Spain was repeated, the "Provincias Internas," of which New Mexico formed a part, were divided into two groups. In order to prevent uncertainty regarding the extent of the constituents of the eastern group, Joaquin de Arredondo, the commandante-general, obtained permission from the viceroy to have official maps constructed of each of the four sections. One of the lines so drawn is of interest in view of later developments. The southwestern and western boundary of Texas was a "zigzag line beginning at the mouth of the Nueces and ending at a point on Red River a little east of the one hundredth meridian of longitude west from Greenwich." [4]

By the Treaty of 1819 between the United States and Spain the northern boundary of the Spanish possessions was definitely established. New Mexico could no longer claim any territory north of 42° north latitude.[5]

New Mexico under Mexico. During the early years of the Mexican regime New Mexico was still one of the Internal Provinces. In January 1824, it was joined to the provinces of Chihuahua and Durango to form the *Estado Interno del Norte.* The location of the capital at Chihuahua was so opposed by Durango that the two southern provinces

3. A Summary of the evolution of the boundaries of the Spanish provinces is given in Prince, *A Concise History of New Mexico*, 14-17.

4. Garrison, G. P., *Westward Extension*, 103-10.

5. Fulmore, Z. T., "History of Texas Geography" in *Tex. Hist. Assoc. Quart.* I, 17; Mallory, *Treaties and Conventions* II, 1652.

were made states and New Mexico became a territory of the Republic. The El Paso district was now joined to Chihuahua; but still no eastern or western bounds were assigned to New Mexico.[6] On the northwest and west the boundary claimed, though not specifically stated, was made by the Colorado River beyond which lay Upper California.[7]

No further changes of any consequence were made previous to the conquest by Kearny; but a number of episodes during the interval had served to crystallize the sentiment of the New Mexicans in regard to the extent of their territory particularly on the east. Here they found that their claims conflicted with those of the young, energetic republic of Texas whose leaders, with true frontier instinct, were loath to have their ambition for westward extension thwarted by a daugher of her whose authority they had repudiated.

Texan Claims. At the first Texas congress an act was passed, December 19, 1836, defining the boundaries of the nation as "Beginning at the mouth of the Sabine River and running west along the Gulf of Mexico three leagues from land, to the mouth of the Rio Grande, thence up the principal stream of said river to its source, thence due north to the forty-second degree of north latitude, thence along the boundary line as defined in the treaty between the United States and Spain to the beginning." [8]

Thus was laid the foundation of the dispute between Texas and New Mexico which eventually involved the members of the congress of the United States in a prolonged, bitter quarrel. For such claims Texas relied, if on anything, on the repudiated treaty which Santa Anna had signed when a prisoner. Texas had never exercised any shadow of juris-

6. Bancroft, *Arizona and New Mexico*, 310-11.
7. Legisl. Journals, Mss. for years 1822-46, 5 v. in Santa Fé Fed. Land Office as cited by Bloom, "New Mexico under Mexican Administration 1821-46," in *Old Santa Fe* I, 13.
8. Laws of the Republic of Texas. 1 Cong., 1 Sess., 133-4 as cited by Binkley, *Texan Efforts to Establish Jurisdiction in New Mexico 1836-1850*, 98.

diction of the territory of New Mexico included in this claim.[9] It was in fact, no more than a claim to be made good by force. As we shall see, she failed decidedly in repeated attempts of such a character.[10]

And yet, when one reads of the desires and even hopes of some of the influential Texans of the times such claims sound modest indeed. Wharton, the commissioner of Texas, in Washington, sent primarily for the purpose of procuring the recognition and annexation of Texas by the United States, reported to his government some time in 1837 that President Jackson had suggested to him that Texas must claim the Californias in order to win over the North and East to the cause of annexation since thereby their fishing interests would be advanced.[11]

The successor of Wharton, Memucan Hunt, became convinced that the officials of the United States desired to extend their boundaries to the Pacific, and he was determined to prevent any agreement which could be interpreted later as implying a relinquishment of this claim on the part of Texas. Writing to his government he stated: "As a separate Power, the splendid harbours on the South Sea, or Pacific Ocean, will be indispensable to us, and apart from the great increase in territory by an extension of the line, the possession of the harbour of St. Francisco alone is amply sufficient, for any increased difficulties or expense, should there be any in regard to a claim of territory to the Pacific, in a final treaty of Peace with Mexico." [12]

Later, when a real effort was inaugurated by Texas for the establishment of peace with Mexico, the commissioner, Dunlap, wrote a private note to President Lamar, May 16, 1839, to ask instructions regarding the propriety of offering a money compensation for the purchase of the land between the Nueces and Rio Grande and continues: "How would you like to have the boundary of the Republic to run to the Paci-

9. Bancroft, *Arizona and New Mexico*, 453-4.
10. Garrison, *Texas*, 263.
11. *Texan Diplomatic Correspondence* II, 285.
12. *Ibid.*, I, 319.

fic so as to include California? This may seem too grasping, but if we can get it ought we not to take it and pay for it?" [13]

Had such ambitions remained but sterile words, they would not belong to our subject; but, in reality, they had a direct bearing on New Mexico. It would appear that the Texans believed that the people of New Mexico would gladly join themselves to their standard if the advantages of such citizenship were but clearly represented to them.

Surely in this case the wish was father to the thought. Texas had been watching the ever increasing prosperity of the trade between Santa Fé and Missouri and greatly desired to divert it to its own territory. This would supply the revenue which was so greatly needed by the young, struggling, Republic whose debt was daily increasing.

The failure of efforts to negotiate a foreign loan and of the plan to establish a government bank caused the Texans to look with envious eye on the income from the Santa Fé-St. Louis trade. President Lamar was convinced that the line of commerce could easily be deflected to Texas. One of the Texan newspapers reported:

> If goods can be landed at Philadelphia, carried overland to Pittsburgh—thence shipped in a steamboat to St. Louis, and again carried overland to Santa Fe, a distance of not less than 1600 miles through almost a desert country and abounding in warlike tribes of Indians, and afford a profit,— how much greater would be the profit to carry them from Texas, less than a third of the distance, and where none of these obstacles exist . . Goods may be landed at Galveston or Linnville, if imported direct from Europe at a cheaper rate than they can be landed at Philadelphia, as our import duty is much less than it is in the United States. From Galveston to Santa Fe is not more than 500 miles— From Philadelphia to Santa Fe it is more than 4000 miles. We have every advantage over the St. Louis trader and only want a little energy to carry the plan into successful operation. [14]

---

13. *Texan Diplomatic Correspondence* II, 385.
14. *Telegraph and Texas Register*, April 8, 1840, as cited in Binkley, W. C., *The Expansionist Movement in Texas*, 1836-1850, 60.

In 1839, President Lamar suggested to the Texan congress the sending of an expedition to New Mexico. He would have commercial relations established between Cuba and Texas with the western terminals of the trade at Chihuahua and Santa Fé.[15] Communications from Texans then in New Mexico gave assurance that the people of New Mexico would gladly welcome annexation to Texas chiefly because of the tyrannical conduct of the governor, Manuel Armijo, who had gained power through a factional revolt. The Texan congress did nothing to forward the plans of Lamar but the latter determined to prepare the way for a peaceful accomplishment of the proposed design.[16]

For this purpose William G. Dryden, when visiting Texas, was instructed to explain to the people of New Mexico the advantages which would accrue to them from union with Texas. It was expected that John Rowland and William Workman, residents of Santa Fé, would coöperate with him. To give an official tone to the commission, the following letter from Abner S. Lipscomb, secretary of state, was sent to the delegates:

It being the intention of his Excellency, the President, shortly to send an expedition to Santa Fe of the Rio del Norte, for the purpose of exploring the best route, and opening a communication with the inhabitants of New Mexico, on the side of the Rio del Norte.—He has instructed me to solicit your aid in communicating with the people of the country and town of Santa Fe, and explaining to them the objects of the expedition.—This Republic claims the ancient boundary of Texas, from the mouth of the Rio del Norte, to its source, and is solicitous, that the civilized inhabitants within its whole limits should be organized under a Government of Laws, securing life, liberty, and property.—Should

---

15. Marshall, T. M., "Commercial Aspects of the Texan Santa Fe Expedition" in *Southwestern Historical Quarterly* XX, 242-259.
16. Binkley, W. C., *op. cit.*, 62-7.

the inhabitants of the North quietly and peaceably organize under our constitution and laws, you can give them the fullest assurance of equal protection and equal rights, privileges and immunities;—that they will be protected in the enjoyment of their religion without molestation or insult to its rights; that there will be no contributions, nor forced loans levied, but that taxation for the support of Government will be uniform throughout the whole Republic, and determined with certainty, not at the will of any officer or officers, but by the Representatives of the people themselves, and that none can be imposed or required in any other mode.—You can assure them that since the battle of San Jacinto, and the defeat and capture of Santa Anna, the progress of improvement in the strength and resources of the Government has been continued uninterruptedly;—that the people are happy under the administration of laws of their own making;—that they are free from all internal commotions; and secure against foreign invasion;—that with harmony of action the interests of the North and the South will become one and the same;—that a relief from a heavy and oppressive import duties will enable them to purchase such articles of merchandise as they may require at a much cheaper rate than heretofore—that the south will be a good market for all their surplus products; that it will be a short and commodious channel of commerce with the European merchants. To the inhabitants of the country known as Pueblo Indians, if they are cultivators of the soil, professing the Christian faith in any form, you may see that they can either come under our laws as citizens, with full and equal privileges, or they can be protected in the full enjoyment of their possessions of land, property and customs, bound only to peace and good order in their relations with the Government. Should it be objected, that Indians under our constitution, cannot enjoy the rights of citizenship in the fullest sense of the term, you are authorized to reply that the term "Indian" as used in our constitution, does not embrace civilized Indians, but applies to the barbarians, only; as by way of illustration many of our citizens of San Antonio county are of the Indian race, but they are civilized, and enjoy equal privileges, and some of them have filled high offices, and some are now members of Congress, and in other offices of honor, trust, and profit. Your acquaintance with the moral conditions of the village Indians, and with our Laws will enable you to determine what position it would best suit them to occupy. It is intended that the expedition shall reach Santa Fe, at farthest by the middle of August. It will be military essentially in its character, but it will be attended by commissioners authorized to propose, and carry out the views of the Government, on the principles I have above expressed. The expedition will be prepared to make a survey of the route, Geological, Mineralogical, and Topographical, and very beneficial results are anticipated. The President is happy in the fortunate circumstance of one of your number being able to speak from his own observation of the operations of our constitution. He will be enabled to inform his associates and others of the result of his experience, and of the salutary influence of our laws. You may assure all the inhabitants that they will be protected in all the rights of property, and every proper precaution taken to prevent any kind of inconvenience or annoyance in the enjoyment of them.[17]

Dissension in the Texas government neutralized these efforts and the contemplated expedition was not authorized by the congress of that year. Lamar did not give up his plans. Without waiting for communication from Dryden regarding his success, but relying on other sources of information, particularly the report that it was believed in Mexico that New Mexico had already joined Texas, he determined to accomplish his design at once. The fear that the Americans then in New Mexico might follow the lead of the Texan revolutionists and set up a Republic of their own, which would more effectively limit Texas than could Mexican control of the region, provided a strong

17. Lipscomb to Dryden, Rowland, and Workman, April 14, 1841, in *Bolton Transcripts.*

incentive at least to Lamar. He determined to act without congress.[18]

Volunteers were requested and merchants were assured that transportation would be furnished and military protection afforded them if they wished to take advantage of this auspicious opportunity to engage in a trading venture.[19]

The plan was widely advertised. Recruits were obtained readily enough. As revealed by letters written later by various members of the expedition, there were various incentives for enlistment. Doubtless the most potent factor was love of adventure as well as curiosity regarding the place of which so much of interest had been reported in preceding years. Since these letters were written after the failure of the enterprise, one wonders if truly an innocent desire to return home to the United States by way of Santa Fé,[20] or pure adventure,[21] or a coveted opportunity of recovering health,[22] together with complete ignorance, especially on the part of the merchants who attached themselves "merely to a military escort through the dangerous Indian country," or an ulterior aim against the government of Mexico on the part of the leaders,[23] could account for the numerous enlistments.

The "Santa Fé Pioneers" as the military force was named, assembled in May at Brushy Creek near Austin.[24] All records and reports of the proposed expedition reveal the assured conviction of the Texans that New Mexico would gladly welcome an opportunity to pledge her allegiance to the Lone Star State. The political and commercial phases seem to have absorbed almost all the attention of those responsible for the enterprise. One of the participants who later wrote the standard account of the whole affair

18. Binkley, *The Expansionist Movement in Texas*, 67-70.
19. *Ibid.*
20. Brenham and Cooke to Thompson, April 22, 1842, in *Bolton Transcripts*.
21. Caldwell to Thompson, April 25, 1842, *Ibid.*
22. Blake to Thompson, April 23, 1842. *Ibid.*
23. Thompson to Bocanegra, May 6, 1842, *Ibid.*
24. General Order No. I, May 24, 1841, in *Order Book of the Texan-Santa Fe Expedition.* Copy in the *Bolton Collection.*

asserts: "The attempt to conquer a province, numbering some one hundred and fifty thousand inhabitants within its borders, was a shade too Quixotical to find favor in the eyes of the three hundred and twenty odd pioneers who left Texas, encumbered with wagons, merchandise and the implements of their different trades and callings."[25]

Specific instructions were given to the commissioners, appointed to organize the government, in regard to the manner of procedure. In case of an armed uprising on the part of the people in conjunction with the Mexican army, a battle was not to be risked. "The President, anxious as he is to have our National flag acknowledged in Santa Fé, does not consider it expedient at this time to force it upon that portion of the Republic."[26] However, if this resistance was only on the part of the Mexican army, the right of possession of Texas was to be enforced.[27]

After taking possession, the commissioners were to appoint to official positions such of the New Mexicans as, in their opinion, were best qualified. These, together with the appointees of the president, would conduct the government in the name of Texas.[28]

Delegates, not more than three, were to be sent by the citizens to the next session of the Texan congress. Their function was evidently that of the minority party in committees. They might observe the Texan methods. They would not be entitled to vote but would probably be allowed to speak on any subject which was of interest to them.[29]

The "Santa Fe Pioneers," the merchants and a few others, together with the supply and merchandise wagons, set out in the latter part of June.[30] The unforeseen diffi-

25. Kendall, G. W., *Narrative of the Texan-Santa Fe Expedition*, I, 16.
26. Garrison, *Diplomatic Correspondence* II, 741.
27. *Ibid.*
28. *Ibid.*, 739.
29. *Ibid.*, 740.
30. Kendall, *Narrative* I, 71-72. For interesting details not recorded by Kendall, see the *Order Book of the Texan Santa Fe Expedition* of which there is a transcript in the *Bolton Collection*.

culties which were encountered and which necessitated a complete change in the manner of advancing are rather surprising. Although the route between Austin and Santa Fé was not entirely familiar in parts, it would seem that more specific information would have been obtained before the final plans were arranged. The time consumed in the march was much longer than had been anticipated.

Preparation in New Mexico. Had hopes been facts perhaps all would have gone well with the optimistic expansionists. But such was not the case. New Mexico was in complete readiness and that readiness meant opposition. Synchronous with the earliest plans of Lamar to initiate the expedition were reports from Governor Armijo to Mexico that such schemes were contemplated. In 1839, the rumor was reported and pressing demands made for the military assistance which the exposed state of the department required. Showing how ridiculously small the military was, he asserted that even a nominal foreign force could wrest New Mexico from the mother country.[31] Although the Minister of War promised assistance in case of actual need,[32] a similar demand for troops was repeated in February of the following year.[33] Armijo declared there were not more than 50 or 60 soldiers in the department. In May he gave reasons for his hostility to the American traders and visitors in the department and asserted that Nait, a naturalized American, had gone from Taos to Texas doubtless for the purpose of acquainting that country with the condition of New Mexico, which had no force to resist foreign encroachments.[34]

In June, more specific information could be given. From Bent's Fort it was learned definitely that a force of Texans was approaching and again Armijo earnestly requested military assistance.[35] This was reiterated in

31. Armijo to Minister of War, August 18, 1839, in *Bolton Transcripts.*
32. Minister of War to Armijo, October 31, 1839. *Ibid.*
33. Armijo to Minister of War, February 4, 1840. *Ibid.*
34. Same to same, May 18, 1840. *Ibid.*
35. Same to same, May 11, 1841, *Ibid.*

July. This time the news had come through travellers to the country of the Comanches. Armijo had given orders not to allow the reported expedition to enter at any point on the frontier. The military were watching all entrance points carefully.[36]

This frontier trouble was taking place when Mexico herself was in a state of turmoil. Yet the determination not to suffer a further diminution of territory is revealed by the promise of the minister of war to send Armijo money with which to raise troops since no soldiers could be sent at that time.[37] But soon Armijo ascertained that the expedition had not materialized and he was able to inform Mexico that his department was in a state of tranquility.[38]

The new year brought a renewal of rumors of hostile activity on the part of Texas and once again the letters giving clear information and appealing for help went from Armijo to the minister of war.[39] These letters reveal how correctly informed the officials of New Mexico were regarding Texan movements.

The governor of Chihuahua, Condé, had also taken an active interest in the rumors. He had been informed by Armijo and by others of the plans which were being formulated. On July 28, 1841, he issued a proclamation to his own people, and forwarded a number of copies to his brother governor to be distributed in New Mexico. It reads:

> I have important news to communicate to you; it is at this moment certain that a band of Texans have begun their march for the purpose of invading this Department or that of New Mexico. Do you know who the Texans are? They are adventurers who despise you as barbarians, weak minded and corrupt men. They blaspheme your religion and scoff at your pious customs; some grasping merchants

36   Same to same, July 12, 1840. *Ibid.*
37. Minister of War to Armijo, July 25, 1840. *Ibid.*
38. Armijo to Minister of War, Sept. 15, 1840. *Ibid.*
39. In the *Bolton Transcripts* there are numberless letters written during this time from Armijo to the minister of war. All have the same general purport.

who envy the fertility of your lands, the richness of your mines, and the clemency of your weather; some, men who distinguish their fellowmen by the color of their faces in order to impress the stamp of slavery on those who are not white; some, fugitives from justice who, coming from different countries, take this name when they arrive in Galveston or pass the Sabine River. Many are those who fight with the savages for your homes; they buy from them the cattle which the latter have stolen from you and supply them with the arms and munitions in order that they may rob you again and cruelly murder you. These are the Texans who, with no other compensation but pillage, no recompense but the possession of the land which they conquer with the sword and despoil with their despotism, attempt not only to maintain the usurpation which their ungrateful predecessors made of a valuable part of the national territory, but also to usurp another greater part and to enrich themselves at the expense of the Mexicans. Their design is, then, to invade and occupy this Department; they approach your frontiers to despoil and enslave you and obliterate with the vile insult of their outrages all the glory of your history.

If, in such circumstances I should have to speak to people whose patriotism was less known to me, to draw back, in their presence, the veil that hides the frightful picture in which are sketched the peculiar misfortunes consequent upon the triumph of the Texans in a struggle whose objects are proprietorship and the liberty of the individuals; in calling together, then, the citizens around the national standard, I should take care to enumerate the abundant means which the supreme government has just put into my hands in order to repel the invaders and that they permit me to arm and equip perfectly the defenders of the nation and to remunerate them with bounty and promptness. Nothing would be exaggerated in this nor anything promised which would not be confirmed very soon by deeds. But I speak with the heroic people of Chihuahua who for hundreds of years have been the strong custodians of the Mexican frontiers and who, in all epochs, have given excellent proofs of their generosity and patriotism. I speak to the people of Chihuahua who, when it is a matter of their religion, independence, and nationality, do not hesitate a moment to rush into the arena to defend interests so precious. Nor do they care to solicit other aid than their own swords, other shields than their own breasts, nor other incentive than their patriotism.

Scarcely, either, would it be necessary for your governors to call you before hand to the conflict; the first boom from the cannon would lead you forth without fail. But I have believed it necessary to direct this address to you in order to warn you against the deceit which precedes the conquerors and travels in the vanguard of all unjust wars. Open the great book of history and you will not find one town that has been subjugated without being first divided by internal discord; on the other hand, neither has human power been capable of overcoming the resistance of a town united and resolved to sustain its liberty.

As the dissensions of Mexico and Tlascala made possible the triumph of the Spanish attack, so the union of the Greeks conquered the formidable army of Xerxes. It is certain that the emissaries of the Texans are already among us and that, by means most indirect, they try to seduce the incautious in order to sow discord among us and to open the way for those who sent them. Let them but deceive one patriot, they will depart and allow the hidden poison to work by itself among those whom they have succeeded in inoculating. Beware then of the seducers and the seduced, whose distinct character consists always in promoting changes and inciting disgusts and complaints. The governor, on his part, promises to watch them with zealous vigilance and punish whosoever may come, thus to manifest the power which the laws have placed in his hands, power which punishes severely the blameworthy at the same time that the report of it terrifies those who might imitate them.

Not being able to deceive the vigilance of the supreme governor completely hiding their hostile purpose, the invaders have taken care to make doubtful the immediate object of their expedition indicating that they are coming to this Department or that of New Mexico without any determined design, or, much less, the points at which they scheme to present themselves. They do this with the intention of dividing our forces, to distract the attention of the authorities and to surprise us asleep in the arms of confidence. Miserable wretches! They have believed that we Mexicans are such as those who are interested in this enterprise describe us. But they make a mistake because in whatever place they present themselves they will find the unfailing resistance which the supreme governor has prepared for them and the inhabitants will oppose them spontaneously. God grant it may be in this department! The people of Chihuahua would, perhaps, be the avengers of the victims of Harrisburg and they would be the first Mexicans to pronounce judgment for those who have suffered heretofore. But if this glory is reserved for the people of New Mexico it remains for us to fight at her side and collect some leaves from her laurels. Yes, New Mexicans, you will see in this department your brothers, the people of Chihuahua, united to you by the strictest bonds; they will help you with all their strength, they will follow, as part of your army, the perfidious Texans from point to point, from redoubt to redoubt and show in all circumstances that all the children of this great nation form but one family, and that this family has sworn to be free and sovereign. . .[40]

By thus giving the impression to the people that the expedition was against them, opposition was effectively developed to any move on the part of Texas to extend control over New Mexico.

Moreover, Armijo neglected nothing which would insure success in the rebuttal of the Texan invaders. Various appointments were made to enable subordinates to assist the governor where such aid was most essential. Antonio Sandoval was instructed to prevent uprisings among the

---

40. Translation of copy of Proclamation in the *Bolton Transcripts*. An original copy is in the Ritch Collection, Huntington Library.

Pueblo Indians,[41] and others were assigned posts on the frontier or among the people.[42] Therefore no move of all the ill-fated "Santa Fé Pioneer" movement came as a surprise. Armijo's forces were at the frontier to meet the exhausted Texans. In two detachments they surrendered without a show of opposition. Their goods were confiscated and they were sent to Mexico on foot, under guard.[43] In Mexico they were imprisoned. Those who could claim that they were not Texans, and many did, were released through the intervention of Waddy Thompson, the minister of the United States to Mexico.[44] Thus ended as a complete failure the expedition undertaken with such high hopes by the "Santa Fé Pioneers." It was evident that New Mexico was not to be claimed by Texas so easily. Later attempts of somewhat similar nature involving, as they did, the interests of different groups, resulted simply in developing ever increasing hostility.[45]

As a department of Mexico, New Mexico looked upon this, however, as a matter to be settled by the Mexican and

---

41. Miranda to Sandoval, Aug. 1, 1841. *Ibid.*

42. See *Bolton Transcripts* for various arrangements of this nature.

43. Kendall, *Narrative* I, 320-340

44. In the *Bolton Transcripts* there are numerous letters to Waddy Thompson written by those who claimed United States citizenship. Notwithstanding the attempted ingeniousness of the communications, Thompson does not seem to have been entirely convinced of the guilelessness of the imprisoned. He based his petition for release, not on the justice of his demand but the good impression such an act of leniency would make on the friends and relatives of the captives who were living in the United States, and the pernicious consequences which would result from continued harshness toward these "Texans." (Waddy Thompson, May 4, 1842, in *Bolton Transcripts*.) Although at first his efforts met with no success, in June 1842, he was able to communicate the following to Daniel Webster, secretary of state: "I have the happiness to inform you that the Texan prisoners were all liberated on the 13th instant. I regard this act of President Santa Anna as one of generosity and magnanimity in every way honorable to him,—and I feel that it is only a matter of justice to the Mexican people to say that their conduct to the prisoners when they were released was kind and generous in the extreme. The prisoners were released upon the parade ground, and when the fact was announced it was received with acclamations by the Mexican soldiers. As the Texans passed through the immense crowd that was assembled, they were most cordially and kindly greeted. When it is remembered that these men had invaded the territory of Mexico, as enemies, such conduct, on the part of the Mexicans is eminently honorable to them." (Thompson to Daniel Webster, June 20, 1842, in *Bolton Transcripts*)

45. Binkley, W. C., *Texan Efforts to Establish Jurisdiction in New Mexico, 1836-1850*, 73.

Texan governments. The question assumed a new phase when Texas became a part of the United States and a still different aspect when New Mexico was thus incorporated.

When news reached Austin of the establishment of a civil government by Kearny, Governor J. P. Henderson wrote to Secretary Buchanan, January 4, 1847, for information regarding the truth of the rumor and whether or not the act had been sanctioned by the United States. He added:

> If General Kearny acted in this matter by authority of the President, and the general government claims the exclusive right of jurisdiction and soil in Santa Fe, I shall, as the Executive of the State, regard it as my solemn duty to protest, in the name of the people and government of Texas, against said act, and claim and reassert the right of Texas to the soil and jurisdiction over that, and all other territory included within her limits, according to the act of Congress referred to above.
>
> Inasmuch as it is not convenient for the State at this time to exercise jurisdiction over Santa Fe, I presume no objectoin will be made on the part of the government of the State of Texas to the establishment of a territorial government over that country by the United States; provided it is done with the *express* admission on their part that the State of Texas is entitled to the soil and jurisdiction over the same and may exercise her right whenever she regards it as expedient.[46]

The reply is rather surprising. After explaining the temporary character of the government set up by Kearny and the necessity of such an act in view of the state of war then existing, Buchanan, at least to some extent, confirmed the claims of Texas by answering:

> . . . Nothing, therefore, can be more certain than that this temporary government, resulting from necessity, can never injuriously affect the right which the President believes to be justly asserted by Texas to the whole territory on this side of the

---

46. *Sen. Ex. Doc. 24*, 31 Cong., 1 Sess., 2.

Rio Grande, whenever the Mexican claim to it shall have been extinguished by treaty. But this is a subject which more properly belongs to the legislative than to the executive branch of the government.[47]

It is not astonishing that the opponents of the administration found in such statements as the foregoing an excellent weapon of attack. If Texas extended to the Rio Grande, from mouth to source, where was the consistency in sending a military force to take possession of Santa Fé, was justly asked. That here was a dilemma no one could gainsay.[48]

During the years of uncertainty, Texas set about making good her claims by actual organization of the territory. On March 15, 1848, the county of Santa Fé was formed.[49] Its boundaries would include practically all of New Mexico contained in the boundary act of 1836. Shortly before, the militia of Santa Fé district was provided for and it was determined to allow it one representative in the Texan congress. The new county was to form the Eleventh Judicial District.[50] Spruce M. Baird was sent as judge.

The report that the Texas legislature planned effectively to extend its control over Santa Fé brought forth a decided protest from New Mexico. The newspaper, *The Republican,* gave warning through its columns that no citizen of the district would ever acknowledge the authority of Texas unless it were ordered by higher authorities; that it would be well to send a bodyguard to conduct their commissioners home safely and intimated that it would be wiser for Texas to drop the matter entirely.[51] Notwithstanding the threatening attitude assumed by this editor, the New Mexicans apparently paid no heed to Baird and he returned to Texas.[52]

47. *Sen. Ex. Doc. 24,* 31 Cong., 1 Sess., 3.
48. See *Congressional Globe,* 29 Cong., 2 Sess., 6-36.
49. Batts, R. L., "Defunct Counties of Texas," in *Texas Hist. Assoc. Quart.,* I, 91.
50. Gammel, "The Laws of Texas," III, 50, 96, as cited by Binkley in *op. cit.*
51. *Niles Register* LXXIV, 224.
52. Davis, W. W. H., *El Gringo,* 110-111.

Another attempt of similar nature was intrusted to Robert S. Neighbors early in 1850. He was instructed to extend the civil jurisdiction of the state over the unorganized counties of El Paso, Worth, Presidio and Santa Fé.[53] Neighbors sent word to the military governor, Munroe, informing him of his commission. Munroe ordered his subordinate officers not to interfere with Neighbors,[54] but the opposition aroused on the occasion was so great that no one went to the polls on the day assigned and one more futile attempt was laid to the account of Texas.[55]

Boundaries Claimed by New Mexico. Perhaps New Mexico took lessons from Texas. At any rate, she too drew up a statement of her boundaries, in true pioneer fashion, at the first State Convention held in 1850. They were to begin at the Rio Grande just north of El Paso and extend thence east to the 100th meridian; thence north along the 100th meridian to the Arkansas river; thence up that stream to its source; thence in a direct line to the Colorado River of the West at its intersection with the 111th meridian; thence south on that meridian to the boundary between the United States and Mexico and along that boundary back to the Rio

---

53. *Sen. Ex. Doc. 67*, 31 Cong., 1 Sess., Worth county was created by Act of January 3, 1850. It was composed of the following territory: "Beginning on the Rio Grande at the northwest corner of the county of El Paso, thence up said river to a point twenty miles above the town of Sabine; thence due to the eastern branch of the Rio Pecos; thence down said stream to the northeast corner of El Paso to the place of beginning." (Batts, R. L., "Defunct Counties of Texas" in *Texas Hist. Assoc. Quart.*, I, 91)

54. *Ho. Ex. Doc. 66*, 31 Cong., 1 Sess.

55. Davis, W. W. H., *El Gringo*, 111. Texas reported the affair to the United States. In a message to the senate, President Taylor, commenting upon it, said that this territory was a portion of that acquired by the war and although he could not take it upon himself to settle the disputed boundary, it should be regarded as debatable land until the question was settled by competent authority. (*Sen. Ex. Doc. 56*, 31 Cong., 1 Sess.)

Later Texas was warned that the entire power of the United States would be employed to prevent any attempt to enforce her authority by arms; that it rested with congress to determine where the true boundary lay and it would be within the competency of that body to offer Texas indemnity for the surrender of her claims if, on investigation, it was convinced that these were well founded. (*Sen. Ex. Doc. 67*, 31 Cong., 1 Sess.)

Grande, down which it was run to the point of the beginning.[56] Just as Texas claimed portions of what was indubitably the Mexican New Mexico so hereby New Mexico, with no stronger basis for the claim than Texas could show, ran her theoretical line well within the limits of the old Spanish Texas. "But it was at last a definite boundary claim on the part of the New Mexican people—the first tangible limits which had ever been named for a province established two hundred and fifty years before."[57]

Claims of Deseret. This claim by New Mexico was directed not only against Texas but also against the newly formed "State of Deseret" or Utah. The Mormons who had settled in "that portion of Upper California lying east of the Sierra Nevada Mountains" were as ambitious as any of the frontiersmen. Early in 1849 a convention was called for the purpose of draughting a constitution whereby they might govern themselves until congress should provide for them. The boundaries set out were as follows:

> . . . commencing at the 33rd degree of north latitude, where it crosses the 108th degree of longitude west of Greenwich; thence running south and west to the northern boundary of Mexico; thence west to and down the main channel of the Gila River, on the northern line of Mexico, and on the northern boundary of Lower California to the Pacific Ocean; thence north to where the said line intersects the dividing ridge of the Sierra Nevada Mountains; thence north along the summit of the Sierra Nevada Mountains to the dividing range of mountains that separates the waters flowing into the Columbia River from the waters running into the great basin; thence easterly, along the dividing range of mountains that separates the waters flowing into the gulf of Mexico from the waters flowing into the gulf of California to the place of beginning.[58]

56. *Sen. Ex. Doc. 74*, 31 Cong., 1 Sess., 2.
57. Binkley, *op. cit.*, 160.
58. Bancroft, *History of Utah*, 441.

Decision in Regard to Claims. Such were the conflicting claims which required adjustment before any definite organization of the new territory could be effected. Of all the claimants, it would seem that Texas had greatest reason to hope that the final decision would be in her favor. But the one vital question to which all others of justice or expediency had to give place was that of slavery. The slave interests would naturally favor the Texas claim, for if its boundaries were acknowledged to extend as far west as was claimed, without more discussion this vast region would be open to slavery; if the New Mexican claims were heard, it would be almost as equally certain that it would be closed to them. Thus only can be understood the mighty conflict which raged in the halls of congress on the apparently simple matter of determining the boundaries of New Mexico.

One circumstance was of powerful assistance in making possible a satisfactory settlement, Texas' debt was assuming alarming proportions. When, therefore, it was asked that Texas give up her claim to the territory within the generally accepted bounds of New Mexico, the proposition received appreciable force when a monetary recompense was offered. After some opposition she finally agreed, November 25, 1850, to accept $10,000,000 for the cession as well as for the relinquishment of ships, revenue from customs houses, etc.[59]

It was thus possible to define the limits of New Mexico as follows:

> Beginning at a point in the Colorado River where the boundary line with the republic of Mexico crosses the same; thence eastwardly with the said boundary line to the Rio Grande; thence following the main channel of said river to the parallel of 32° north latitude; thence east with said degree to its intersection with the 103° longitude west of Greenwich; thence north with that degree of longitude west of Greenwich; thence running south and west with that parallel to the summit of the Sierra

59. Message of President Fillmore, Dec. 13, 1850, Richardson, V. 108-9.

Madre; thence south with the crest of those mountains to the thirty-seventh parallel of north latitude; thence west with said parallel to its intersection with the boundary line of the state of
California; thence with said boundary line to the
place of beginning.[60]

Running the Southern Boundary. While these decisions
were being reached, arrangements were being made for
compliance with Article V of the Treaty of Guadalupe-
Hidalgo which provided:

The boundary line between the two republics
shall commence in the gulf of Mexico, three leagues
from land opposite the mouth of the Rio Grande
otherwise called Rio Brave del Norte, or opposite
the mouth of its deepest branch, if it should have
more than one branch emptying directly into the
sea; from thence up the middle of that river, following the deepest channel where it strikes the
southern boundary of New Mexico; thence west-
wardly, along the whole southern boundary of New
Mexico (which runs north of the town called Paso)
to its western termination; thence northward along
the western line of New Mexico until it intersects
the first branch of the river Gila. . . The southern
and western limits of New Mexico, mentioned in
this article are those laid down in the map entitled
"Map of the United Mexican States", as organized
and defined by various acts of the Congress of said
republic and constructed according to the best
authorities. Revised edition. .Published at New
York in 1847 by J. Disturnell. . ."

In order to designate the boundary line with
due precision, upon authoritative maps and to
establish upon the ground landmarks which shall
show the limits of both republics as described in

---

60. *Legislative Blue Book of New Mexico*, 36. "That part lying west of longitude 109° was detached in 1863 to form Arizona; and that part above 37° in 1867 [1861]
was attached to Colorado. There was also a large addition in 1854 by the Gadsden Purchase, most of which was detached with Arizona. Utah as organized in 1850 included
the later Nevada, Utah, and those part of Colorado and Wyoming which lie south of
latitude 42° and west of the mountains. There was a little strip of territory
acquired from Mexico lying between latitude 38°, the mountains, and the Arkansas
River, that does not seem to have been provided for in the final settlement of 1850."
(Bancroft, *Arizona and New Mexico*, 458)

the present article, the two governments shall each appoint a commissioner and a surveyor, who, before the expiration of one year from the date of the exchange of ratifications of this treaty shall meet at the port of San Diego and proceed to run and mark the said boundary in its whole course to the mouth of the Rio Bravo del Norte. . .[61]

On the part of the United States, John B. Weller was appointed first commissioner, Andrew B. Gray, first surveyor, Major Emory, astronomer, and John C. Cremony, interpreter.[62] On the Mexican commission were Don Pedro Garcia Condé, commissioner, and José Salazar y Larregui, surveyor and astronomer.[63] The commissioners assembled at San Diego in June and began work as soon as possible. The task was made extremely difficult because of the lure which was being held out by the recently discovered gold fields of California. Men could not be obtained as escorts and to perform the laborious work at the low and uncertain wages offered by the government, while the prices of all the necessities of life were rising beyond all precedent. Repeatedly the work was all but rendered impossible by these conditions.[64]

In the latter part of 1849, an agreement was reached in regard to the initial point of the boundary near San Diego. The point of junction of the Gila and Colorado was then determined. There was no difficulty in locating the line between the two points. It was then found to be impracticable to advance eastward beyond the mouth of the Gila towards the frontier of New Mexico.[65] It was then decided to meet at El Paso. The commission was reorganized and Bartlett replaced the dismissed Weller, June 19, 1850.[66]

61. *Ho. Ex. Doc. 69*, 30 Cong., 1 Sess.

62. Bartlett, J. R., *Personal Narrative* I, 2.

63. *Sen. Ex. Doc. 119*, 32 Cong., 1 Sess., 56, 59.

64. Emory, *Report* I, 1-5.

65. Bartlett, *Personal Narrative* I, 1-5. The work of the commission was rendered almost impossible because of the play of politics in the appointment and dismissal of commissioners, etc., and the failure to provide funds. This lies beyond the scope of this work. See *Cong. Globe*, 31 Cong., 2 Sess., pp. 78 *et seq.*

66. *Sen. Ex. Doc. 119*, 32 Cong., 1 Sess., 87.

In December, 1850, the first meeting of the reorganized joint commission took place at El Paso. Meetings were held as regularly as possible, twice a week.[67] Difficulties at once presented themselves. According to the terms of the treaty, the Disturnell map was to be used as a basis of the negotiations. But the errors in this map rendered a satisfactory agreement almost impossible. The Rio Grande was located more than two degrees too far east and the town of El Paso about half a degree north of the 32d parallel while its true position is a degree farther south. It was finally decided "to fix the Initial Point on the Rio Grande at the latitude given by the map without any reference to where the true line so prolonged should terminate. Therefore, according to this determination, the point where the middle of the Rio Grande strikes the Southern Boundary of New Mexico is 22' of arc north of the parallel of latitude marked 32° upon the map. From the same point thence the Southern Boundary of New Mexico extends 3° to its Western termination."[68]

Although Bartlett had thus conceded some territory which might justly be claimed, he felt that he had gained more than he had lost. When the agreement was reached, the official surveyor, Gray, was not present. On his arrival late in July, 1851, he found the monument indicating the initial point already laid and the running of the southern boundary of New Mexico begun. He refused to recognize the agreement and recalled Whipple who was acting surveyor. Discussions between the members of the commission and the play of politics in congress still further retarded the work. Finally it was intrusted to Major Emory under whom better results were achieved. By December, 1853, the survey was completed.[69]

Dissatisfaction with the Boundary. The boundary decided upon did not meet with the approval of congress.

67   Bartlett, *Narrative* I, 145-151.
68.   Bartlett, *ibid.*, 202-3. *Sen. Ex. Doc. 119*, 32 Cong., 1 Sess., 238.
69.   *Sen. Ex. Doc. 119*, 32 Cong., 1 Sess., 279-291, 116, 119. Emory's *Report* I, 15; Rippy, J. F., *The Relations of the United States and Mexico, 1848-1860*, 168.

Many looked to the commissioners so to establish the line that a practicable southern route for a Pacific railway woud be gained. It was felt that this had been sacrificed by placing the boundary of New Mexico too far north. Furthermore a flourishing settlement had been begun in the only fertile region in the otherwise desert strip under dispute. This district, known as La Mesilla, had been populated by the Mexican element of Doña Ana in 1849-50. Some few Americans had also gone there. Their motive cannot be definitely determined in view of the conflicting accounts. Bartlett attributes it to the exasperation caused by the encroachments of the Americans and the determination of the Mexicans to retain their Mexican citizenship; while from reports to the governor of New Mexico it can be inferred that the settlers clearly understood, in establishing their new homes, that they would be within the boundaries of the United States. Evidently there was a division of the people, some desiring the northern, some the southern jurisdiction. Doubtless the choice was guided by original citizenship.[70]

As soon as it was definitely settled by the boundary commission that the disputed area was in Chihuahua, its chief executive took measures legally to incorporate the region. Those "favorable to American rights and privileges" objected and petitioned the governor of New Mexico to lay their complaint before the federal government.[71]

William Carr Lane, the successor to Calhoun in New Mexico, on hearing that the federal government had repudiated the line established by Bartlett went in person to Doña Ana and by proclamation laid claim to the disputed territory. Trias, the governor of Chihuahua, refused to admit the claims of Lane, and maintained that the inhabitants whose citizenship would be thus eventually determined did not desire annexation to the United States. He gave

---

70. Rippy, op cit., 176 ; Bartlett, op. cit., 291-2.
71. Rippy, op. cit., 178.

warning that, if necessary, he would defend the rights of his nation by force.

Although Lane was at first inclined to respond with force, circumstances caused him to change his tactics. The military commander of New Mexico refused to grant assistance in enforcing his proclamation, and, moreover, the minister of the United States in Mexico on being informed on the matter advised Lane to "gracefully" change his attitude.

Shortly after, the federal government showed its apparent disapproval by appointing Meriwether to supersede Lane. Meriwether was informed of the "error" made by the boundary commission but was instructed to "abstain from taking forcible possession of the tract even if on your arrival in New Mexico you find it held adversely to the claim of the United States by Mexico or the authorities of Chihuahua."[72]

Notwithstanding the seemingly conciliatory attitude adopted by the United States, there was a strong wave of apprehension throughout Mexico. Periodicals of the time, doubtless influenced by Santa Anna, expressed indignation at the grasping policy of the United States. The fear and anger were increased by excerpts from editorials in American newspapers which advocated the absorption of more Mexican territory.[73]

The Gadsden Treaty. The final result of the disagreement was the treaty concluded on December 30, 1853, by James Gadsden, United States minister to Mexico.

The instructions to Gadsden have never been made public but there is much reason to think that he endeavored to obtain a large strip of Mexican territory including a large part of Chihuahua and all of Lower California. Santa

---

72. Marcy to Meriwether, May 28, 1853. State Dept. B. U. A. Ms., as cited by Rippy, *Texan Efforts to Establish Jurisdiction in New Mexico*, 184.
73. Rippy, *op. cit.*, 188-195.

Anna took to himself the honor of reducing the amount granted to about half of the demand.[74]

Article I as finally agreed upon provides:

> The Mexican republic agrees to designate the following as her true limits with the United States for the future: retaining the same dividing line between the two Californias as already defined and established, according to the 5th article of the treaty of Guadalupe-Hidalgo, the limits between the two republics shall be as follows: Beginning in the Gulf of Mexico, three leagues from land, opposite the mouth of the Rio Grande, as provided in the 5th article of the treaty of Guadalupe Hidalgo; thence, as defined in the said article, up the middle of that river to the point where the parallel of 31°47' north latitude crosses the same; thence due west one hundred miles; thence south to the parallel of 31°20' north latitude; thence along the said parallel of 31°20' to the 111th meridian of longitude west of Greenwich; thence in a straight line to a point on the Colorado River, twenty English miles below the junction of the Gila and Colorado rivers; thence up the middle of the said river Colorado, until it intersects the present line between the United States and Mexico. . .[75]

$10,000,000 was paid to Mexico, then greatly in need of money, and the United States gained undisputed title to the desired route for a railroad to the west.[76]

Major Emory was appointed United States commissioner and surveyor. He worked harmoniously with the Mexican appointees, José Salazar y Larregui and Francisco Jiménez, and the survey and marking of the boundary were completed before the end of October, 1855.[77]

74. Wharton, R. G., *The Gadsden Treaty*, Santa Anna, *Mi Historia Militar y Politica*, 106-111.

75. *Ho. Ex. Doc. 109*, 33 Cong., 1 Sess., 2.

76. The results of recent investigations on this subject are found in Garber, P. N., *The Gadsden Treaty;* Rippy, J. F., "A Ray of Light on the Gadsden Treaty" in the *Southwestern Historical Quarterly*, XXIV; and "The Negotiation of the Gadsden Treaty," in volume XXVII of the *Quarterly*.

77. Bancroft, *Arizona and New Mexico*, 491-4. Emory, I, 26-36.

The boundaries of New Mexico were now definitely settled on north, south, east, and west. These far flung lines were later contracted in various ways, but for the present there was no reason for uncertainty regarding her true limits.

CHAPTER VIII

THE FIRST YEARS OF TERRITORIAL GOVERNMENT

Provisions of the Organic Act. By the Organic Act, passed by congress on September 9, 1850, and approved in December by President Fillmore, New Mexico became a territory of the United States. According to the decrees of this act the legislative power and authority of the territory were vested in a governor and a bicameral legislature. The council, consisting of thirteen members, was to be elected for two years and the house of representatives of twenty-six members for one year. Universal suffrage by male citizens twenty-one years of age was provided. The governor, secretary, attorney, marshal, and three justices of the supreme court were to be appointed by the president, by and with the consent of the senate. The governor, was, ex-officio, superintendent of Indian affairs. This would give an emolument of $1000 in addition to his salary of $1500 as governor. Salaries of the officials were to be paid by the United States. All acts passed by the legislature and signed by the governor had to be submitted to, and receive the approval of, congress before becoming effective.[1]

First Legislative Assembly. The first legislative assembly was opened on June 2, 1851. According to a contemporary who lived long enough to be able to judge in perspective, the first was the best legislature the territory ever had; it counted in its personnel the finest Mexicans and Americans that the region could produce.[2] A study of the acts passed bears out the praise accorded.[3] It is impossible to learn from whom or what group much of this legislation emanated.

Among the chief of these provisions was the incorporation of the City of Santa Fé,[4] which was made the capital.

---

1. *Legislative Manual,* 34-41
2. Ellison, S., *History of New Mexico,* 17. (Ms.) [This was edited by J. Manuel Espinosa, in N. M. HIST. REV., Jan'y 1938.]
3. See *Ho. Mis. Doc. 4,* 32 Cong., 1 Sess.
4. This was repealed in the following session.

According to the old Spanish mode, its boundaries were defined as lying in each direction one mile from the centre of the plaza.

New Mexico was divided into three judicial districts and appropriations were made for the taking of the census by counties.[5]

Congress was requested to reserve the wood and timber on the mountains and all other untillable lands for the common use of the people and forbid its sale or individual appropriation. The same provision was requested for the salt mines and salt springs.

In order to prevent litigation, and because of the familiarity of the people therewith, it was also petitioned that the laws of Mexico on mines and mining be declared and perpetuated.

It was shown how essential it was that provision be made at once by congress for roads, especially from Taos to Santa Fé. For this purpose an appropriation of $50,000 was requested. The memorial, explaining the justice of this petition, is a valuable description of the condition of New Mexico at the time. It states that of the vast extent of the territory, the valleys alone were inhabitable and these were separated from one another by large stretches of desert land. "It resembles more a string of settlements than a regularly populated country."[6] The need for roads was most felt at Taos, a prosperous agricultural region without access to any market for the sale of its products. The road so opened would greatly facilitate military operations and thus yearly would save the government as much as the initial cost. New Mexico was doomed to a long disappointment on this score.

Judging from ores and outcroppings that the country contained great mineral wealth in copper, gold, silver, lead,

---

5. The returns of the first census showed 61,457 residents in New Mexico. Of this number 538 were persons born in the United States. This did not include those connected with the army. (*Cong. Globe App.*, 32 Cong., 1 Sess., *Ho. of Rep.* 335)

6. *Ho. Mis.. Doc. 4*, 32 Cong., 1 Sess., 15.

and quicksilver, as well as coal, iron and gypsum, the legislators requested congress to provide for a geological and mineralogical survey. Assurance of the presence of these minerals would, they said, induce capitalists to locate there which would promote the enterprise and interests of New Mexico. The geologic survey would also reveal the practicability of artesian wells which "would make the present barren fields fertile" and thus induce settlement.

A problem requiring federal decision was that of those Mexican citizens who had, according to the treaty of Guadalupe-Hidalgo, retained their Mexican citizenship but who now wanted to be naturalized as Americans. Since there was no law on this subject, congress was petitioned to formulate one.[7]

The first governor. James S. Calhoun, who was appointed the first governor, had been in New Mexico as Indian agent since 1849. According to practically all the accounts given of him he was very popular with the Mexican population and those Americans who had a vested interest in the region. Judge Baker, one of the American judges, writing of him stated that he was justly entitled to the confidence of the people on account of the extreme care he took of their welfare and his desire to make the recently conquered Mexicans feel they were American citizens entitled to all the rights and privileges of citizens of the United States. He made an effort to appoint the more eminent and influential of them to those offices which he considered them capable of filling. This antagonized many of the Americans who evidently had hoped to profit politically and financially by the new regime.[8]

At all events he met with such opposition that almost all his efforts for the peace and prosperity of New Mexico were paralyzed. His relations with the military officials were so strained that there was no effective coöperation, to the great detriment of the country which consequently

---

7. *Ho. Mis. Doc., 4,* 32 Cong., 1 Sess.
8. Calhoun, *Correspondence,* 408.

suffered more from Indian depredations than it had ever suffered before. The history of the first years of American control of this former Mexican outpost are not of a nature to flatter the American sense of superiority.

Indian outrages. While Calhoun was Indian agent, before being named governor, he wrote to Orlando Brown, the commissioner of Indian affairs in Washington:

> "Reports of 'all's well' and that our difficulties are being overcome and that there ought to be no changes in the affairs here; that the people are happy and contented and prosperous . . . such reports can emanate only from luxurious ease, stupid ignorance, or combinations whose interest it is to perpetuate the present state of things which Mr. St. Vrain and others, long residents of this country, pronounce to be worse than any they have ever witnessed before—and I assure you they are infinitely worse than you can imagine."[9]

On July 9, 1851, the members of the legislature addressed Governor Calhoun on the conditions. They stated that New Mexico was in a deplorable condition due, primarily, to Indian depredations and that at the time of writing they did not possess one tenth of what they had possessed in previous years. In 1830-34 the country presented a scene of great prosperity when over a million and a half heads of sheep and cattle roamed over the plains affording a large commerce with the United States and Mexico. Previous to 1851 the governors and dictators paid no attention whatever to the remonstrances of the people since there was no legal constitution on which to base claims. Governor Calhoun was requested to garrison the frontiers of the country in order to prevent the incursions of the savages.[10]

There are two possible explanations of the continuance of this state of affairs after the establishment of territorial

---

9. Calhoun, *Correspondence*, 142.
10. Calhoun, *Correspondence*, 386-7.

government. One is insufficient funds;[11] the other, much more plausible, the antagonism between the civil and military officials as well as between two factions of the people. The "state party" is accused of doing everything possible to stir up animosity against Calhoun and his supporters.

Speech of Mr. Weightman in Congress. In the annals of the discussions which took place in congress during the eventful years immediately following the passage of the Compromise of 1850 is found a lengthy speech of R. H. Weightman, representative of New Mexico, which, although primarily of a political nature, indicates rather clearly the underlying reasons for such disorder.[12]

The appointment of Calhoun as first governor met with the approval of the delegate and he asserted that the support tendered by the people to the new administration was chiefly due to the fact that it differed so essentially from that of the person previously in control, Colonel Munroe. Against the latter, Mr. Weightman preferred very serious and seemingly well-founded charges of wilful neglect of duty and failure to provide for the guaranteed rights of the people of New Mexico, such as freedom of religion and prompt legal trials of accused according to due forms of law.

In a glowing eulogium of his constituents, Mr. Weightman asserted that Governor Calhoun agreed with him in believing "that the people of New Mexico are capable of self-government. . . that they are not the miserable, degraded, and vicious people that they have been represented to be by the adherents of the . . . military government."[13] He insisted that the presence of the troops in and around Santa Fé was desired by the traders and merchants, of whom the majority were Americans, on account of the business they assured. This group was opposed to Governor Calhoun because, besides other causes for disaffection, at his arrival the troops were transferred to frontier posts.

---

11. *Ibid.*, 306.
12. *Cong. Globe. App.*, 32 Cong., 1 Sess., 322-336.
13. See *Sen. Ex. Doc. I*, 32 Cong., 2 Sess., pt. II.

Mr. Weightman averred that the resident Mexicans together with the comparatively few Americans who had established themselves permanently in Santa Fé and who were, therefore, more anxious for peace and order than a market for goods rejoiced in their removal and gave unqualified support to the new governor.

A citation from the press of October 28, indicated the commercial effects of the removal of the troops.

> Santa Fe is dull, very dull,—dull in the superlative degree. The headquarters of the army have been removed from here to a place . . . somewhere north of Barclay's fort. Money seems to have taken flight with the army. The glory of Santa Fe has departed, I fear me, forever. I yesterday was told by one of the chief merchants of the place that for the last twenty days he had not paid expenses. But the hope of better times is entertained by us all and gives us some comfort,

The frequent reports of civil dissension in New Mexico on the part of the Mexican population were declared emphatically to be the inventions of political agitators. As a proof of the exaggeration in the stories of "revolts and anarchy, confusion and revolution" the speaker challenged anyone to cite and substantiate a single instance in which resistance had been offered to the execution of the laws, since the treaty of peace.

If the representative of the people of New Mexico knew whereof he spoke, and there is little reason to doubt his knowledge, the frequent reports of murders and depredations of Americans were either grossly exaggerated or entirely fictitious or directly traceable to serious fault on the part of Americans. In support of his assertion he states:

> Of all those who have been loudest in their outcries that there was no safety for American lives in New Mexico, what two have thought it necessary to come together for the purpose of combining for self-defense? In the midst of all this outcry . . . there has been no case of a native citizen of the United

States fleeing, for fear of his life, from his place of business in New Mexico. They are living now and have been all the time in perfect security; living in whatever town in New Mexico interest or freak dictated—in many cases a single one living in a town where, for months at a time, he could converse in the English language—living with New Mexicans without its ever occurring to them to fear the consequences of doing so, except, theoretically, when passing resolutions for political effect . . . I have never met in any part of the United States people more hospitable, more law-abiding, more kind, more generous, more desirous that a general system of education should be established among them . . . Among them I have met gentlemen of incorruptible integrity, of honor, refinement, intelligence and information . . .[14]

Attempts to discredit the territorial government. Efforts were made by the faction in opposition to Governor Calhoun to arouse antagonism against him on religious grounds. The *Santa Fe Gazette,* August 1851, contained an article entitled "The Triangular Fight between the Military, the Judiciary, and the Catholic Church." [15] Governor Calhoun was quite certain that its object was to convey a false impression of a transaction which was evidently of a perfectly innocuous nature but which would certainly be misinterpreted if some of the facts were suppressed. Therefore he gave his official approval to the following complete statement of the episode.

When Judges Mower and Watts arrived in Santa Fé from St. Louis, June 1851, they took up their residence with the governor. The group antagonistic to the governor refused to call at his house to pay their respects to the judges. Attempts were made to win the judiciary to the side

---

14. *Cong. Globe. App.,* 32 Cong., 1 Sess., 322-336. Of an entirely contrary tenor is the report made by Colonel Sumner, in charge of the military, to the secretary of war, May 27, 1852. He had nothing of good and much of evil to record concerning the New Mexicans. It is quite evident that he was greatly disaffected toward the people he was appointed to protect. For his views see *Sen. Ex. Doc. 1,* 32 Cong., 2 Sess., pt. II.

15. *Cong. Globe. App.,* 32 Cong., 1 Sess., 325.

of the disaffected group but an emphatic statement was issued to the effect that the judiciary would not take any part in political matters. Mr. Sherman, clerk of the district court of Judge Mower, in reporting the affair to Judge Baker asserted that the members of the first legislative assembly under the Organic Law "hailed with unfeigned delight the arrival of the judges as an omen of a better state of things; they having the utmost confidence in the civil government of the Territory and of the United States; looking upon the Judges and the Executive with great veneration, being themselves law-abiding people and appearing very anxious to conform to the customs and laws of the United States." It was therefore the ambition of the opposing faction to secure the influence of the judges on their side. With the judiciary and the military in agreement against the governor the latter would be helpless.

Failing in this attempt, because of the refusal of the judiciary to take part in politics, the ring-leaders hit on a scheme by means of whch to render the judiciary unpopular with the people by making it appear that these officials would interfere with their religion.

The opportunity was found in the circumstances attending the holding of a court session soon after the arrival of the judges. Arrangements were first made to hold the session in the Quartermaster's quarters. Shortly before the date set for the opening of court, Colonel Baker, in command of the military, refused to allow the rooms to be put to that purpose. He stated that under certain specified conditions he would allow the use of one of the old churches which had been under the control of the army ever since the conquest.

While preparations were under way for fitting the edifice for the purpose, Bishop Lamy, appointed to the Santa Fé diocese shortly after the establishment of American control in New Mexico, called on the judges and claimed title to the church. After a completely amicable discussion in which it was shown that since the army claimed control the question should be referred to the district attorney, Bishop Lamy quietly consented to file the claim to ownership as suggested. The matter would have rested thus, until official investigation of the title deeds, had not the opponents of the governor used the episode to persuade the people that this was an unwarranted attack on their religious liberty. Finding that real bitterness was being developed, the judges decided to find some other building and did so the next day. In expressing his opinion on the subject Bishop Lamy said that the people had doubtless been wrought upon for some political purpose. Many had come to him to know whether or not they should resist the holding of the court in the church. He replied that under no circumstances would he approve the raising of a finger against the civil authorities. He used his influence to persuade them to go home and remain quiet.[16] Thus the second organized attempt to discredit Governor Calhoun was a failure.

These continued wranglings were most disastrous to New Mexico. Although in isolated cases military aid was accorded to the governor in order to enable him to show force against the Indians, such assistance was too sporadic to be really effective. Moreover he frequently complained that instructions from Washington were entirely too few to enable him to achieve the best results.[17]

Ill health finally caused Governor Calhoun to seek in a visit to "the States" at least temporary relief from his arduous duties. He left in charge of the Indian office John Greiner who thus epitomizes his position:[18] "Left in charge of the superintendency of Indian Affairs by Governor Calhoun, without a dollar to pay expenses, without any means provided to meet any of the Indians, with only one Indian

16. Calhoun, *Correspondence*, 406-11.

17. Calhoun, *Correspondence*, 414. Under most favorable conditions mail was delivered only once a month from Independence. It took six weeks for a letter to reach New Mexico from the Atlantic Seaboard. Mail was also delivered monthly from San Antonio, Texas. (Davis, W. W. H., *El Gringo*, 272). On Feb. 5, 1851, a petition bearing sixty-four signatures was drawn up for a semi-monthly mail (Alvarez Papers)

18. Governor Calhoun died on his way east before reaching Missouri. Friend and political foe alike mourned one who had certainly done much to insure American control in New Mexico.

agent in the Territory and he in the Navajo country, with a rumor that the Comanches are forming a league with the other wild tribes to pounce down upon New Mexico and Texas, with suspicions that some devilment is afoot among the Pueblos, with rumors of revolution among the Mexicans, with the Governor, Secretary, and Chief Justice absent in the States you can judge of my position." [19]

Yet the same person reported in August 1852 that matters were gradually adjusting themselves and that there was great reason to hope that soon the story of distress and turmoil would be changed into one of peace and prosperity. After riding over nearly the whole Territory "from the Arkansas to the Gila Rivers and from Acoma to Antoine Chico" he could say what could never be said before that the Indians were all at peace.[20] Though short-lived, this era of tranquility was of great benefit to the people.

Internal Development. It is extremely difficult to determine to what extent American interest was manifested in the internal development of New Mexico. Apart from the trade with both east and west which had long before passed the experimental stage, the chief attraction was the reputed mineral wealth. That mining was begun early under American auspices is beyond question. A communication of August 1851 affirms that work had been going on in the gold mines near Santa Rita de Cobre. "The country here, from the Rio Grande to the Rio Gila cannot be surpassed by any other part of New Mexico, and the mines all about here are very

---

19. "Correspondence of J. G." in *Journal of American History* III, 552. The letters of John Greiner give an interesting, intimate picture of life in New Mexico. The writer gives little credit to the soldiers in controlling the Indian situation but explains that it was not ill-will but inability which made them so ineffective. He says: "There are 92,000 Indians (estimated) in this Territory. Many of them are at war. We have not 1,000 troops here under Colonel Sumner to manage them. Our troops are of no earthly account. They cannot catch a single Indian . . . Heavy dragoons on poor horses who know nothing of the country, sent after Indians who are at home anywhere and who always have some hour's start . . . So far, although several expeditions have started after them, not a single Indian has been caught." (*Ibid.*, 549)

20. Polk, *Diary*, Sept. 30, Oct. 3, 1848.

rich in Gold, Silver, Copper, lead, etc., etc.; in Gold I do not suppose that California can surpass it." [21]

Although this is, doubtless, too enthusiastic, the mineral deposits were recognized as readily valuable. Greiner stated that news came in to the Americans at Santa Fé of gold and silver being found in various localities. He was confident that there was much silver near Taos.[22]

Some development was made in the arts of peace even during the years of turmoil. The territorial library was established in 1852 by means of an appropriation of $5,000 made by congress in 1851. A later addition of $500 to defray the expense on transportation of books made possible the library loans without which the so-called library would be scarcely more than an empty building.[23]

Reference has already been made to the interest of the people in education and the petition sent to congress in one of the earliest memorials from New Mexico for appropriations for that purpose. Although this was not granted, private initiative provided the desired facilities. On January 1, 1853 the Convent of Our Lady of Light was opened by the Sisters of Loretto whom Bishop Lamy had succeeded in persuading to come to New Mexico to aid him in the work of education of the children under his charge.[24]

In almost all the other regions which became parts of the United States there were public lands which could be procured so easily that immigration rapidly followed annexation. This was not the case in New Mexico where, during

---

21 Calhoun, *Correspondence*, 419. The purpose of the letter was to obtain military aid against the Apaches and Navajoes who threatened to make impossible the continued operation of the mine.

22. "Correspondence of J. G." in *Journal of American History*, III, 547-548.

23. Ellison, S., *History of New Mexico* (Ms), 19. Before 1856 it contained 2,000 volumes, "standard text books on various branches of common and civil law and equity, the reports of the U. S. and state courts and codes of various states and territories, besides a number of congressional documents." (Davis, *El Gringo*, 171-2)

24. An excellent account of the opening of the Academy of Our Lady of Light Academy, Santa Fe" by Sister M. Lilliana Owens in *New Mexico Historical Review*, XIII, No. 2, 129-145 (April, 1938)

the long Spanish and Mexican regimes, all the desirable land had been occupied.[25]

This and the California gold rush prevented the rapid influx of Americans. Gradually, however, the conquering race dominated; the trader had not come in vain; New Mexico became American.

Conclusion

The American occupation of New Mexico was the resultant of a number of forces acting in the same direction. The trappers and traders aroused general interest throughout the United States in the commercial advantages which would accrue from possession of this nearby foreign land; federal administrators viewed with enthusiastic approval the prospect of extension of control to the Bay of San Francisco by the acquisition of intermediate territory; slavery and anti-slavery interests each recognized therein a promising field for the establishment of its respective system with the consequent regaining of threatened political ascendancy in congress; Texas saw the desirability of rounding out her dominions by expansion to the "natural frontier," the Rio Grande.

Had diplomacy been able to accomplish its purpose, New Mexico might peacefully have become part of the United States. Mexico, however, failed to grasp the viewpoint of her ambitious northern neighbor; and, although financially embarrassed to the point of bankruptcy, refused to cede her distant province in exchange for claims lodged against her. Nor could she be persuaded that it would be to her own best interest to accept a money compensation for land that was of no apparent benefit to her, and was much desired by another. Repeated failure to effect the cession revealed that here was a region in which century-old ownership and "manifest destiny" would inevitably clash before the latter could come into her own.

When the conflict ensued, New Mexico was not mentioned as a determinant factor. But the early official interest in the "Army of the West" reveals irrefutably the attitude of the administration toward New Mexico. Where negotiation failed, the sword succeeded.

The interests of New Mexico, during the first years of

25. The conflict between the original owners and the "squatters" was long and bitter. The account of the final settlement by the Court of Private Land Claims established in 1891 lies outside the scope of this work.

American domination, were subordinated to more pressing problems of national scope, to the great detriment of the conquered region. Its very distance from the centre of national life put it at a great disadvantage; neither slavery nor anti-slavery would allow its rival to establish itself in the land conquered by the sacrifices of the sons of both factions.

Under such circumstances, it is not strange that the control of the Indian population, most vital to New Mexico, was not adequately provided for, nor the adjustment of problems of government given due consideration. How these and other matters of engrossing importance commanded adequate national concern, and how, by the successful endeavors of her residents, New Mexico eventually became in fact, as well as in name, an integral part of the nation, belong to a later history of the United States.

BIBLIOGRAPHY

PRIMARY MATERIAL

I. United States Government Publications

American State Papers, 12 vols. Wait Pub. Boston, 1819.

American State Papers, Military Affairs IV. Wash., 1860.

Congressional Globe

Vol.	III	24 Cong., 2 Sess., 1836-1837
Vol.	XVII	29 Cong., 2 Sess., 1846-1847
Vol.	XIX	30 Cong., 1 Sess., App., 1847-1848
Vol.	XX	30 Cong., 2 Sess., 1848-1849
Vol.	XXI	31 Cong., 1 Sess., 1849-1850
Vol.	XXII	31 Cong., 2 Sess., 1850-1851
Vol.	XXIII	31 Cong., 2 Sess., 1850-1851
Vol.	XXV	32 Cong., 1 Sess., App., 1851-1852
Vol.	XXVI	32 Cong., 2 Sess., 1852-1853

House Documents

24 Cong., 1 Sess., Doc. 256.
Correspondence between the United States and Mexico, 1835-1836.

24 Cong., 2 Sess., Doc. 2.
Message of President Jackson, Dec. 1836, with accompanying documents between the Dept. of State and Gorostiza.

24 Cong., 2 Sess., Doc. 105.
Message and correspondence regarding the relations between the United States and Mexico and the condition of Texas, 1836-1837.

25 Cong., 1 Sess., Doc. 42.
Message and correspondence regarding the boundary between the United States and Mexico, 1824-1838.

25 Cong., 2 Sess., Doc. 351.
Message and correspondence regarding the relations between the United States and Mexico, 1828-1838.

27 Cong., 3 Sess., Doc. 166.
Message and correspondence in relation to the taking possession of Monterey by Commodore T. A. C. Jones.

28 Cong., 1 Sess., Doc. 2.
Correspondence on the annexation of Texas.

29 Cong., 2 Sess., Doc. 19.
Correspondence in regard to the occupation of Mexican territory. Contains the Organic Law for the territory of New Mexico compiled under the direction of Gen. Kearny.

30 Cong., 1 Sess., Doc. 60.
Message and correspondence on the Mexican War.

30 Cong., 1 Sess., Doc. 69.
Message and documents on the treaty with Mexico.

30 Cong., 1 Sess., Doc. 70.

Message on California and New Mexico.
30 Cong., 1 Sess., Doc. 76.
Message and correspondence in relation to the number of Indians in Oregon, California, and New Mexico, and the military force necessary.
30 Cong., 2 Sess., Doc. 1.
Message and correspondence relating to civil government in California and New Mexico, 1848.
31 Cong., 1 Sess., Doc. 5.
Reports on conditions in the Southwest.
31 Cong., 1 Sess., Doc. 17.
Message and correspondence on affairs in New Mexico containing the report of Charles Bent on the Indians in New Mexico.
31 Cong., 1 Sess., Doc. 66.
Claims of Texas to Territory in New Mexico.
31 Cong., 1 Sess., Doc. 39.
Journal of Convention held at Santa Fe.
31 Cong., 1 Sess., Doc. 220.
Report on credentials of W. S. Messervy.
32 Cong., 2 Sess., Mis. Doc. 4.
Acts, resolutions and memorials of legislative assembly of Territory of New Mexico, 1851.
33 Cong., 1 Sess., Doc. 109.
Gadsden Treaty of Dec. 30, 1853.

Senate Documents

24 Cong., 1 Sess., Doc. 400.
Message and correspondence on the depredations by Mexicans on the property of Chouteau and Demun.
28 Cong., 1 Sess., Doc. 341.
Treaty between the United States and Texas with accompanying correspondence.
30 Cong., 1 Sess., Doc. 1.
Message of President Polk, Dec., 1847, with accompanying documents.
30 Cong., 1 Sess., Doc. 7.
Notes of a military reconnoissance made in 1845-7 by W. H. Emory.
30 Cong., 1 Sess., Doc. 26.
Memoir of a tour to northern Mexico connected with Colonel Doniphan's Expedition in 1846 and 1847 by A. Wislezenus.
30 Cong., 1 Sess., Doc. 52.
Treaty with Mexico, with Senate proceedings.
31 Cong., 1 Sess., Doc. 24.
Correspondence on the boundary of Texas.
31 Cong., 1 Sess., Doc. 60.
Information regarding the formation of a state government in New Mexico.
31 Cong., 1 Sess., Doc. 74.
Constitution adopted by New Mexicans in 1850.

31 Cong., 2 Sess., Doc. 1 pt. II.
Correspondence on the subject of civil affairs in New Mexico.

31 Cong., 2 Sess., Doc. 26.
Colonel McCall's report of 1850 in regard to New Mexico.

32 Cong., 1 Sess., Doc. 71.
Report of the Secretary of War in relation to civil officers employed in the Territory of New Mexico while under military government.

32 Cong., 1 Sess. II, pt. 1, Doc. 2.
Report on Indian and Military Affairs, 1851.

32 Cong., 1 Sess., Doc. 119.
Papers on the Mexican Boundary Commission.

32 Cong., 1 Sess., Doc. 121.
Report of Lieut. Col. Graham on the subject of the boundary line between the United States and Mexico.

32 Cong., 2 Sess., Doc. 1, pt. 1.
Report on the boundary of New Mexico.

32 Cong., 2 Sess., Doc. 1, pt. 2.
Report on Military Dept. of New Mexico by Col. Sumner, 1852.

32 Cong., 2 Sess., Mis. Doc. 36.
Memorial from New Mexican Leg. on Pacific railroad.

II. OTHER PRIMARY MATERIAL

Abel, A. H., ed.
The Official Correspondence of James A. Calhoun while Indian Agent at Santa Fe and Superintendent of Indian Affairs in New Mexico. Washington, 1915.

Adams, J. Q.
Speech of—upon the rights of the people to petition, etc. Delivered in the House of Representatives June 16 to July 7, 1838. Washington, 1838.

Archives of New Mexico. *Manuscripts.*

Barreiro, A.
Ojeada Sobre Nuevo Mexico, Puebla, 1832.

Bartlett, J. R.
Personal Narrative of Explorations and Incidents in Texas, New Mexico, California, Sonora, and Chihuahua. 2 Vols. N. Y., 1854.

Boggs, Thos.
Dictations, 1885. (*Ms. in Bancroft Library*)

Bolton Collection of Transcripts from the Principal Archives of Mexico. (*Mss. University of California*)

Bolton, H. E.
Guide to Materials for the History of the United States in the Principal Archives of Mexico. Washington, 1913.

Breevort, E.
The Santa Fe Trail. (*Ms. in Bancroft Library*) 1884.

Brown, Joseph C.
"Field Notes by—, United States Surveying Expedition 1825-1827" in *Eighteenth Biennial Report of the Board of Directors of the Kansas State Historical Society,* Topeka, 1913.

Cooke, P. St. George
  The Conquest of New Mexico and California. N. Y., 1878.
Coues, E., ed.
  The Expedition of Zebulon Montgomery Pike, 3 vols. N. Y., 1895.
  The Journal of Jacob Fowler. N. Y., 1898.
Cutts, J. M.
  The Conquest of California and New Mexico, Phil., 1847.
Davis, W. W. H.
  El Gringo or New Mexico and Her People. N. Y., 1857.
Dublan, M., y Lozano, J. M.
  Legislacion Mexicana, Tomo I, Mexico, 1876.
Garrison, G. P., ed.
  "Texas Diplomatic Correspondence," in *Annual Report of the American Historical Association,* 1907. Vol. II.
Gregg, J.
  Commerce of the Prairies. 2 vols. N. Y., 1844.
Greiner, J.
  "Correspondence of," in *A Journal of American History,* III. New Haven, 1909.
Historical Society of New Mexico. *Manuscripts.* Santa Fe.
Hughes, J. T.
  Doniphan's Expedition . . . Cinn., 1847.
Kendall, G. W.
  Narrative of the Texan Santa Fe Expedition. 2 vols. N. Y., 1844.
Malloy, W. M., comp.
  Treaties, Conventions, International Acts, Protocols and Agreements between the United States of America and Other Powers, 1776-1909, 2 vols. Wash., 1910.
Mexico, Secretaria de Relaciones Exteriores
  La Diplomacia Mexicana. 3 vols. Mexico, 1910-1913.
  Tratado de Amistad, Commercio, y Navegacion entre los Estadoes Mejicanos y los Estadoes de America. Mexico, 1832.
Moore, J. B.
  History and Digest of the International Arbitrations to Which the United States Has Been a Party. 6 vols. Wash., 1898. (Also printed as *Ho. Mis. Doc. 212,* 53 Cong., 2 Sess.
Niles.
  National Register. 75 vols. Baltimore-Philadelphia, 1811-1849.
Pike, Z. M.
  Exploratory Travels (edited by T. Rees). London, 1811.
Pino, P. B.
  Noticias Historicas y Estadisticas, de la Antiqua Provincia del Nuevo-Mexico . . . 1812 *(Adiconadas por el Lic. D. Antonio Barreiro en 1839, y Ultimamente Anotadas por el Lic. Don Jose A. de Escudero).* Mexico, 1849.
Quaife, M. M., ed.
  The Diary of James K. Polk. 4 vols., Chicago, 1910.
Richardson, J. D., ed.
  Messages and Papers of the Presidents, 10 vols. Washington, 1902.

Ritch, W. G.
  The Legislative Blue Book of the Territory of New Mexico. Santa
  Fe, 1882.
  Ritch Collection of Manuscripts in Huntington Library.
Santa Anna, A. L. de.
  Mi Historia Militar y Politica, 1810-1874. Mexico, 1905.
Twitchell, R. E., ed.
  The Spanish Archives of New Mexico. 2 vols. Cedar Rapids,
  1914.
Walker, Joel P.
  Narrative of Adventures (Ms. in Bancroft Library.)
Willard, Dr.
  "Inland Trade with New Mexico," in *Personal Narrative of J. O.
  Pattie.* (Flint ed.) Cinn., 1833.
Wizlizenus, A.
  *Memoir of a Tour to Northern Mexico, connected with Col. Doni-
  phan's Expedition, in 1846 and 1847.* Washington, 1848.

SECONDARY MATERIAL

Bancroft, H. H.
  Arizona and New Mexico. S.F., 1889.
  History of Utah. S.F., 1889.
Batts, R. L.
  "Defunct Counties of Texas" in *The Quarterly of the Texas State
  Historical Association* I, 1897-1898.
Benton, B.
  "The Taos Rebellion" in *Old Santa Fe* I, 1913.
Benton, T. H.
  Thirty Years' View, 2 vols. N. Y., 1852-56.
Binkley, W. C.
  The Expansionist Movement in Texas, 1836-1850, Berkeley, 1925.
Binkley, W. C.
  "The Question of Texan Jurisdiction in New Mexico under the
  United States, 1849-1850" in *The Southwestern Historical Quar-
  terly,* XXVI.
  "New Mexico and the Texas Santa Fe Expedition" in *The South-
  western Historical Quarterly,* XXVII.
Bloom, L. B.
  "New Mexico under Mexican Administration, 1821-1846," in *Old
  Santa Fe,* vols. I-III. 1913-16.
Bolton, H. E.
  *Athanase de Mezieres and the Louisiana-Texas Frontier, 1768-
  1780.* 2 vols. Cleveland, 1914.
  "French Intrusions into New Mexico," in *The Pacific Ocean in
  History.* N. Y., 1917.
  Texas in the Middle Eighteenth Century. Berkeley, 1915.
Bolton and Marshall.
  The Colonization of North America, 1492-1783. N. Y., 1920.
Brooks, M. C.
  A Complete History of the Mexican War. Phil., 1849.

BIBLIOGRAPHY 163

Brown, M. A.
Federal Indian Policy in New Mexico, 1846-1851.
(M.A. Thesis in Univ. of Cal., 1917.)

Chittenden, H. M.
The History of the American Fur Trade of the Far West. 3 vols.

Cox, I. J.
"The Southwest Boundary of Texas," in *The Quarterly of the Texas State Historical Association,* VI, 1902-3.

Davis, W. W. H.
El Gringo or New Mexico and Her People. N. Y., 1857.

Fulmore, Z. T.
"History of Texas Geography," in *The Quarterly of the Texas State Historical Association* I, 1897-98.

Garber, P. N.
The Gadsden Treaty, Phil., 1923.

Gerrard, L. H.
Wah-to-Yah and the Taos Trail. N. Y., 1850.

Garrison, G. P.
Texas, a Contest of Civilization. Boston and N. Y., 1903.
Westward Extension, 1841-1850. N. Y., 1903.

Hill, J. J.
"The Old Spanish Trail," in *Hispanic American Historical Review,* IV, Aug., 1921.

Hodge, F. W., ed.
Handbook of American Indians North of Mexico. 2 vols. Washington, 1907.

Houck, L.
The Spanish Regime in Missouri. 2 vols. Chicago, 1909.

Klein, J.
The Making of the Treaty of Guadalupe-Hidalgo on February 2, 1848. Berkeley, 1905.

Kohl, C. C.
Claims as a Cause of the Mexican War. N. Y., 1914.

Manning, W. R.
Early Diplomatic Relations between the United States and Mexico. Baltimore, 1916.

Marshall, T. M.
A History of the Western Boundary of the Louisiana Purchase, 1819-1841. Berkeley, 1914.
"Commercial Aspects of the Texan Santa Fe Expedition," in *The Southwest Historical Quarterly,* XX, 1916-1917.
"St. Vrain's Expedition to the Gila in 1826," in *The Pacific Ocean in History,* edited by Stephens and Bolton. N. Y., 1917.

McCormac, E. I.
James K. Polk, a Political Biography. Berkeley, 1922.

Prince, L. B.
A Concise History of New Mexico. Cedar Rapids, 1912.
Historical Sketches of New Mexico from the Earliest Records to the American Occupation. Kansas City, 1883.
History of New Mexico. Kansas City, 1883.

164 AMERICAN OCCUPATION OF NEW MEXICO

New Mexico's Struggle for Statehood, Sixteen Years' Effort to Obtain Self Government. Santa Fe, 1910.

Read, B. M.
Illustrated History of New Mexico. Santa Fe, 1912.

Reeves, J. S.
American Diplomacy under Tyler and Polk. Baltimore, 1907.

Rippy, J. F.
The Relations of the United States and Mexico, 1848-1860. (Unpublished doctoral thesis in Univ. of Cal. Library.)
"A Ray of Light on the Gadsden Treaty," in *The Southwestern Historical Quarterly,* XXIV.
"The Negotiation of the Gadsden Treaty," in *The Southwestern Historical Quarterly,* XXVII.

Rives, G. L.
The United States and Mexico, 1821-1848. N. Y., 1913.

Ruxton, G. F.
Wild Life in the Rocky Mountains. N. Y., 1916.

Sabin, E. L.
Kit Carson Days (1809-1868). Chicago, 1914.

Smith, J. H.
The War With Mexico. 2 vols. N. Y., 1919.

Thomas, D. Y.
A History of Military Government in Newly Acquired Territory of the United States, N. Y., 1904.

Territory of New Mexico.
Report of the Secretary of the Territory 1909-1910 and Legislative Manual, 1911. Santa Fe, 1911.

Twitchell, R. E.
The Leading Facts of New Mexican History. 5 vols. Cedar Rapids, 1911.
The Military Occupation of New Mexico. Denver, 1909.

Tyler, L. G.
The Letters and Times of the Tylers. 2 vols. Rich., 1885.

Wharton, R. G.
The Gadsden Treaty. (M. L. Thesis in Univ. of Cal., 1912.)

INDEX

THE CHICANO HERITAGE

An Arno Press Collection

Adams, Emma H. **To and Fro in Southern California.** 1887

Anderson, Henry P. **The Bracero Program in California.** 1961

Aviña, Rose Hollenbaugh. **Spanish and Mexican Land Grants in California.** 1976

Barker, Ruth Laughlin. **Caballeros.** 1932

Bell, Horace. **On the Old West Coast.** 1930

Biberman, Herbert. **Salt of the Earth.** 1965

Casteñeda, Carlos E., trans. **The Mexican Side of the Texas Revolution (1836).** 1928

Casteñeda, Carlos E. **Our Catholic Heritage in Texas, 1519-1936.** Seven volumes. 1936-1958

Colton, Walter. **Three Years in California.** 1850

Cooke, Philip St. George. **The Conquest of New Mexico and California.** 1878

Cue Canovas, Agustin. **Los Estados Unidos Y El Mexico Olvidado.** 1970

Curtin, L. S. M. **Healing Herbs of the Upper Rio Grande.** 1947

Fergusson, Harvey. **The Blood of the Conquerors.** 1921

Fernandez, Jose. **Cuarenta Años de Legislador:** Biografia del Senador Casimiro Barela. 1911

Francis, Jessie Davies. **An Economic and Social History of Mexican California** (1822-1846). Volume I; Chiefly Economic. Two vols. in one. 1976

Getty, Harry T. **Interethnic Relationships in the Community of Tucson.** 1976

Guzman, Ralph C. **The Political Socialization of the Mexican American People.** 1976

Harding, George L. **Don Agustin V. Zamorano.** 1934

Hayes, Benjamin. **Pioneer Notes from the Diaries of Judge Benjamin Hayes, 1849-1875.** 1929

Herrick, Robert. **Waste.** 1924

Jamieson, Stuart. **Labor Unionism in American Agriculture.** 1945

Landolt, Robert Garland. **The Mexican-American Workers of San Antonio, Texas.** 1976

Lane, Jr., John Hart. **Voluntary Associations Among Mexican Americans in San Antonio, Texas.** 1976

Livermore, Abiel Abbot. **The War with Mexico Reviewed.** 1850

Loyola, Mary. **The American Occupation of New Mexico, 1821-1852.** 1939

Macklin, Barbara June. **Structural Stability and Culture Change in a Mexican-American Community.** 1976

McWilliams, Carey. **Ill Fares the Land:** Migrants and Migratory Labor in the United States. 1942

Murray, Winifred. **A Socio-Cultural Study of 118 Mexican Families Living in a Low-Rent Public Housing Project in San Antonio, Texas.** 1954

Niggli, Josephina. **Mexican Folk Plays.** 1938

Parigi, Sam Frank. **A Case Study of Latin American Unionization in Austin, Texas.** 1976

Poldervaart, Arie W. **Black-Robed Justice.** 1948

Rayburn, John C. and Virginia Kemp Rayburn, eds. **Century of Conflict, 1821-1913.** Incidents in the Lives of William Neale and William A. Neale, Early Settlers in South Texas. 1966

Read, Benjamin. **Illustrated History of New Mexico.** 1912

Rodriguez, Jr., Eugene. **Henry B. Gonzalez.** 1976

Sanchez, Nellie Van de Grift. **Spanish and Indian Place Names of California.** 1930

Sanchez, Nellie Van de Grift. **Spanish Arcadia.** 1929

Shulman, Irving. **The Square Trap.** 1953

Tireman, L. S. **Teaching Spanish-Speaking Children.** 1948

Tireman, L. S. and Mary Watson. **A Community School in a Spanish-Speaking Village.** 1948

Twitchell, Ralph Emerson. **The History of the Military Occupation of the Territory of New Mexico.** 1909

Twitchell, Ralph Emerson. **The Spanish Archives of New Mexico.** Two vols. 1914

U. S. House of Representatives. **California and New Mexico:** Message from the President of the United States, January 21, 1850. 1850

Valdes y Tapia, Daniel. **Hispanos and American Politics.** 1976

West, Stanley A. **The Mexican Aztec Society.** 1976

Woods, Frances Jerome. **Mexican Ethnic Leadership in San Antonio, Texas.** 1949

Aspects of the Mexican American Experience. 1976

Mexicans in California After the U. S. Conquest. 1976

Hispanic Folklore Studies of Arthur L. Campa. 1976

Hispano Culture of New Mexico. 1976

Mexican California. 1976

The Mexican Experience in Arizona. 1976

The Mexican Experience in Texas. 1976

Mexican Migration to the United States. 1976

The United States Conquest of California. 1976

Northern Mexico On the Eve of the United States Invasion:
Rare Imprints Concerning California, Arizona, New Mexico,
and Texas, 1821-1846. Edited by David J. Weber. 1976